Rope Saw

Rope Saw

The Remarkable Journey
Learning to Use a Rope Saw

Floyd Roland Park

Books Press

First Edition
Books Press December 2024
Manufactured in the United States of America
ISBN 979-8-9921405-0-7

Dedicated to those who are wise
enough to seek counsel and humble
enough to heed it.

Disclaimer

This book is intended for entertainment purposes only. It is not intended for instruction how to trim trees or use a Rope Saw. Techniques, methods, procedures, or activities, described in this book are not recommended. Tree trimming is a dangerous activity and should only be completed by professional tree trimmers. If you need a tree trimmed, call a professional. Neither the publisher nor the author shall be liable for any loss of profit or any personal or commercial damages; including, but not limited to special, incidental, consequential, personal, or other damages claimed to originate from information in this book.

Contents

Illustrations

Illustrations

Illustrations

Photographs

Photographs

Photograph   Page

1
The Challenge

I was confronted with a major challenge. The cotton wood tree in my backyard was slowly dying. The tree was over sixty feet tall and it had several leafless branches that were perilously positioned over my house and garage. I was concerned one of the branches would break off and do extensive damage.

I had no experience trimming trees, so I asked my Dad what he thought I should do about the dead branches. Dad was always my go-to when I had an important decision to make. He was intelligent and his wisdom and advice was always solid. Looking back, it was foolish of me not to always follow his advice.

I told Dad about the dead branches and my concern that they could break off and damage the house. Dad never missed a beat; he told me not to do anything; if a branch fell on the house, let the insurance company deal with it.

Mom on the other hand was willing to learn and try almost anything.

Forty years ago, she convinced Dad to quit his job and buy a gas station. The plan was to convert the gas station into a convenience store. The were no convenience stores at the time and no one I knew had ever heard of one. When they told us kids what they were planning to do, we thought they flipped out and we would end up supporting them. But Mom knew what she was doing, and the idea turned out to be good.

I have always liked to learn new things like my Mom did. I am generally willing to try almost anything. Mom had a knack for putting things together logically before trying them. Her logic was always good, and she knew the difference between a wild idea and one that was not.

That is not necessarily true of me. Wild ideas are my forte. You can ask my friends. I generally view everything as doable; no matter how wild of an idea it is. I remember something Anthony Hopkins said in the movie *The Edge, directed by Lee Tamahori.* He said that "What one man can do; another can do." That saying stuck with me and I have used it to justify some pretty stupid ideas.

I have a fear of heights. When I must go on the roof of my house, I seldom stand. Crawling on all fours seems much safer to me and I do not care what the neighbors think. The tree was over sixty feet tall and many of the branches that needed trimming were high in the tree. That being the case, I knew that I would not be able to trim the tree myself, so I called a professional tree trimmer. In retrospect, hiring a professional was my most intelligent choice.

The professional tree trimmer arrived within a day or two. I will refer to him as Jed, which is not his real name - I am not protecting the innocent - I am still just a little miffed at the size of the estimate. Anyway, I liked Jed, but as we stood in my backyard gazing at the tree, all Jed could do for the first five minutes was say, "Man, that's a big tree." I agreed with Jed that it was a big tree, but I knew exactly where the whole thing was leading. The only thing I could be thankful for, at that point, was that he was planning to mail the estimate to me instead of telling me on the spot, which would have resulted in Jed and me no longer being friends.

As we continued to look up at the tree, Jed made several comments about having to get insurance, and how his men would have to climb the tree and how dangerous it would be for them, what a big job it would be, and how long it would take. Jed also thought the branches were in imminent danger of breaking off and, if they did, they could do catastrophic damage to the house, garage, and my billfold.

As Jed continued analyzing the work that was needed to remove the tree, he explained that I would need to remove a thirty-foot fence in the backyard as well as a permanent awning over the patio in order to give him access to the tree and to keep the awning from being damaged. I quickly analyzed the work needed to remove the fence and the awning. Neither would be easy, and the work would take weeks to do. Additionally, I did not have any more experience removing fences or awnings than trimming trees.

I thanked Jed for coming, we shook hands, and he left. I hoped Jed did not notice how sweaty my hands were. April is cool where I live, and sweaty palms are almost unheard of. My palms do not normally sweat unless I get incredibly nervous. Jed gave me the distinct impression that the bid was going to be high. It did not help my sweaty palms when he said he would put the estimate together as quickly as possible since he thought the tree was such an imminent safety threat.

Two days later I got the startling news; five-thousand dollars. I announced the grand total of the bid to my wife, who knows less about trees than me, if that is possible. Surprisingly, she just kept on preparing supper, like it was no big deal.

The bid was high; so high Jed apologized for it. The tree was big, and his bid matched the tree. Honestly, the bid would have been higher if I were bidding to cut the tree down myself. I knew it would be a ton of work. Unfortunately, I believed I could find a better way to take care of the tree, and I would not have to take the fence or awning down to do it. The only challenge was to find the better way.

As we slowly worked our way through the supper dishes, the gears in my head turned ceaselessly as I searched for a solution to the tree dilemma. By the time I finished the dishes, I realized the gears needed more grease, so I went out to stare at the tree. I believe if you stare at a problem long enough, the solution to the problem will come. I have used this approach uncountable times in my life and I can say with one hundred percent confidence that it has almost never proven true. What happens is that an idea comes to mind that is about a nine on the wild idea scale. For unknown reasons, it is never obvious to me that an idea is wild until I get deep into it. My first idea was at least a nine.

Looking up at the tree, I realized that the challenge was to cut branches off without leaving the ground. I figured I could somehow overcome my fear of heights, but I would have to do it while standing on a ladder using a chain saw. It seemed to me that hanging onto a chain saw while balancing on a ladder would not mix any better than gasoline does with sparks. So, leaving the ground was out of the question.

I am not known for my carpentry ability. I would be the first to say my projects always turn out very poorly, which is an understatement. Anyone who has seen my carpentry work would agree. I once made a quilt rack for my Mom. I will never forget the look on her face when she first saw it. She ended up piling so many quilts on it that there was no way you could see the rack. Years later the quilt rack mysteriously disappeared. I have often wondered what happened to it. My folks did not have a fireplace. I was glad it was gone so Mom did not have to deal with it anymore.

I have an electric chain saw. No, I am not one of those "green" people, I just did not want a gasoline powered one because they seem dangerous. I cannot explain why an electric chain saw is less dangerous, it is just a feeling I have; proving again that feelings mean nothing. I have always opted for less dangerous power tools because it makes good sense. The electric saw is dangerous, but it is a pole saw that extends twelve feet. Keeping the saw twelve feet away from my appendages works for me.

I am fortunate to have a private fenced-in backyard. It is really both a blessing and a curse; it is a blessing because no one can see me doing anything wild, and it is a curse because, since no one can see me doing anything wild, I do more wild things.

I am extremely poor at judging distances. When I buy rope or electric extension cords, they are always too short. Thinking twelve feet was a significant distance for a saw to reach, I went out and extended the saw to the full twelve feet to evaluate my theory. The extended saw was about ten feet short of the lowest branch that I needed to trim. Using my elevated level of deduction, I concluded that I would somehow need to extend the saw more than twelve feet.

I got my eight-foot stepladder out of the garage. I set the ladder up, grabbed the pole saw, and ascended the ladder to the fifth rung. I extended the pole saw to its full length and immediately felt the sensation of being very unbalanced. Thinking the sensation could be random, and finding I was short of reaching the branch, I went up two more rungs. At that point I realized the unbalanced sensation was not random. Trying to steady the pole saw while on the stepladder was something only a circus acrobat could do.

Compared to most garages, my garage is in good order. I know where all the stuff is supposed to be, so it usually does not take me too long to find where it is. The thing I like most about my garage is finding stuff I did not know I had.

I have cleaned out my garage since, but it used to be a wild-idea-parts-heaven. I used to keep anything I thought might come in handy someday. I had a wide variety of stuff, but I always found it necessary to modify the stuff I had, to make it useable for any given wild idea.

Looking through the stuff, all I found were two boards that were eight feet long. An eight-foot extension would not be long enough, but sixteen feet would be.

In my head, where I usually do my mental stuff, I visualized connecting the two boards with pipe clamps. They would need to overlap a little, which would reduce the overall distance gain, but I did not have longer boards to work with, so they would have to do.

The people at the hardware store know me well. We get along good because they never ask any questions. I never ask any questions either, since asking questions can generate rebuttal questions that might inadvertently expose me and thereby make it impossible for me to revisit the hardware store in the future. I bought the clamps without incident. I am sure they thought I was working with pipes.

After returning home with the clamps, I figured I had a couple hours to work before supper, which would give me enough time to test my idea and get all the evidence put away. I was able to attach the saw to the first board. It was a little trickier to attach the two boards together. As they say, there is strength in numbers, and it applies to pipe clamps too. I don't remember how many pipe clamps I used, I do remember that I was glad no one could see the boards spliced together; it was not pretty.

Everything spliced together resulted in a twenty-six-foot pole saw. To get power to the saw, I wrapped the leading thirty feet of a one-hundred-foot extension cord around the homemade pole. Realizing that I would need to somehow push two buttons on the saw to turn it on, I devised a way to push the buttons using wood clamps. The downside to using the wood clamps was that the saw would be running as soon as I plugged it in, so I would need to position the saw on the branch where I wanted to cut it, then plug the saw in. This setup seemed to be a little dangerous, but I could not think of another way to do it.

My extended pole saw was ready, and I had a solid plan in place to test it. I strategically snaked the electrical cord through the yard so I could plug it in in the garage. Everything looked good.

As I started to lift the contraption skyward toward the branch, a single thought popped into my head; "heavy." I do not mean "heavy" as in profound, although the weight of the contraption was profound, the saw, with two eight-foot boards, unnumbered pipe clamps, a couple wood clamps, and a good length of electrical cord, made the weight difficult to ignore. However, at that point in the test, I decided that I was too far along to abort, so I decided to ignore the weight and continue with the test.

It took effort to lean the contraption in the crotch of the tree. Then with even more effort I moved the saw from the crotch of the tree to the place where I wanted to cut. I rested the pole saw on the ground while moving it because it weighed too much for me to hold. While moving the pole it reminded me of how the poles flex that the circus trapeze people carry. I struggled to move the saw as it swayed side to side uncontrollably. Scary moments later, I was able to get the saw to rest against the four-inch-thick test branch I wanted to cut off. I was careful to put the non-moving part of the saw against the tree because otherwise, after the saw was plugged in, it would jump wildly out of control.

I double checked to make sure I was ready to continue, which required a little creative thinking. With apprehension, I plugged the saw in. The whining saw quickly became unsettling and caused me to be less focused than I should have been. Instead of smoothly transferring the saw from the resting position to the cutting position, the saw began to sway uncontrollably away from the branch.

I rely heavily on providence, which is what I began to do as I struggled with the unwieldy, overweight, wildly whining and swaying, twenty-six-foot contraption. Only providence allowed me to safely rest the saw at a point in the tree where it would not do anything damaging or dangerous while I sprinted to the garage and unplugged it.

After the somewhat hair raising experience, I needed a time out. Reviewing the data I mentally collected from the test, I deemed the Extend-Pole-Saw-With-Boards idea a no go. The deciding factor was that the contraption was too unstable, too heavy, and just plain dangerous. The only good thing about the test was that no one saw me hideously attempting to balance the contraption. Had there been witnesses, not only the test would have been deemed unstable and dangerous, I would have been too. I slowly and gently lowered the contraption to the ground, dismantled it, and stored all the parts back in the garage. It would be difficult to describe my project as going smoothly at that point. But I was not going to be deterred from the mission at hand.

As I go over my experiences trimming the tree using a Rope Saw, you will see that tree trimming was a high-risk activity. It was stressful, dangerous, and physically demanding. The Rope Saw is a great tool that was useful for removing small branches. Larger branches presented a greater risk. I always followed the instructions that came with the Rope Saw and I never stood directly under a branch I was cutting.

I subsequently used, what I call a Security Line, to ensure my safety. The Security Line kept the Target Branch from falling to the ground after I cut it free from the tree.

Although the Security Line could have failed, the chance was minimal if I connected the Target Branch to the Security Line correctly. I never stood directly under the branches I cut and I never had a Security Line fail.

The key to my safety was proper preparation and mindfulness of what a branch could do after I cut it free from the tree. In reality, there was no way for an amateur like me to know what a branch would do. I should have called a professional to trim the tree.

2
Learning the Ropes

When I set my mind to something I cannot let it go until I finish what needs to be done. It is not a good trait. I feel fortunate that I did not start jumping stuff with motorcycles. I can imagine seeing a ridiculous jump challenge and thinking there must be a way to jump over it. Before you know it, I would be strapping a rocket to my motorbike and hitting the switch. Now that I think about it, Evel strapped a rocket on. Me and Mr. Knievel must be alike. I wonder if he ever did any tree trimming.

It took me a while to produce another idea. First, I tried walking through the hardware store looking for an idea, but the ideas there were either non applicable or were ideas that did not apply to tree trimming in any way. So, I went straight to the top of the wild idea food chain, the Internet. After searching for a while, something called a pocket camp saw came up. The saw was like a twelve-inch wire. The wire was like a coping saw blade with a ring at each end. It was easy to see how a camper would use this type of saw to cut down small trees and branches. They could then use them to build a shelter, a fire, or whatever campers build with small trees and branches. I could see a possibility here and, after my experience with the saw extension system, I wanted to check it out some more. There were a couple of problems with the camping saw. It would not be long enough to go all the way around larger branches and I had no idea how fast it would cut a branch. The saws were not expensive and I thought I could hook two together for cutting larger branches. The greatest thing about finding the camping saw was the advertisement. In the ad they referred to the camping saw as a Rope Saw. I had never heard of a Rope Saw before.

I have been gifted with the ability to create words. One word I created is hooliganaster. I created it right after graffiti artists decorated my garage for the third time. I experienced another hooliganaster just three weeks ago when a graffiti artist mistook my fence for a train car.

Another word I thought I invented was discombobulate. Shortly after I invented it, I heard someone use the word on the radio. I was shocked to hear it. I was amazed that my word caught on so fast. I almost called the radio station to claim royalties or threaten a lawsuit, but I searched and found the word listed in an old dictionary.

Seeing the term "Rope Saw" was exciting because it gave me something new to search the Internet for. Before the Internet bloomed, searches needed to be specific or you did not get any hits. For example, if you search for "saw", then the only hit you got was a saw, and that was it. Today, if you search saw, you get saw, seen, looked, Stihl and four million two hundred thousand other things that match. I searched for "Rope Saw" and got one hit. The hit was for a professional high limb Rope Saw.

I opened the advertisement. It appeared promising. I was particularly happy to see "High Limb" in the name. The picture was worth a thousand words, it showed that the Rope Saw was a serious version of the camp saw. It was longer and had the same type of blade that is on chain saws.

It was obvious that the Rope Saw is intended for professionals. I am sure there are professional tree trimmers that would use a Rope Saw, especially if they are afraid of heights like me. It is easy to visualize a tree trimming service truck pulling up to the house and a big burly tree trimmer jumping out of the truck carrying a Rope Saw. The ad did not limit the purchase of a Rope Saw to only professionals, so I read on.

Speaking of professionals, a while back I took my Rope Saw into the local chain saw shop to get it sharpened. They had never seen one before. It makes me think that they either never actually saw one, or they would not admit that they have seen one, which I can understand. I think most people who use chain saws are people who like to fish, which means they inherently have a problem with telling the truth. I go fishing, but anyone who knows me will tell you that what I do is not actually fishing. I mostly just sit on the shore and look around. Which explains why I have a real problem with not telling the truth.

The ad described two Rope Saw options. There was a twenty-four inch for twenty-nine dollars, and a forty-eight inch for forty-nine dollars. Please do not quote me, when working on wild ideas I seldom consider the cost. Wasting money seems to be an integral part of my wild ideas. It is odd, because all my wild ideas are supposed to save money. They say you must spend money to make money. In my case, you must waste money to save money.

The ad also showed a man on the ground with the Rope Saw looped up around a branch. I particularly liked to see the man standing on the ground. I think the ad department was likely the same one who created the ad for the Red Rider BB Gun. The Rope Saw was perfect. I was more than willing to fork over forty-nine dollars for a saw. I could not wait for it to arrive.

It would be several days before the Rope Saw was delivered, so I was on a Rope Saw holiday. I was relaxed, stress free, and confident knowing a solution to the tree was on the way. I knew the tree was about to get what is coming to him, or her. I guess trees are male and female, but I have no idea how to tell. Which reminds me of one of my first wild ideas when I was just a kid - raising rabbits.

When I was a kid, I got two rabbits to raise as pets. I liked my rabbits, but I did not understand the birds and bees. I am not sure I understand it yet. Anyway. I started with two rabbits which quickly increased to twenty-something (they were coming so fast I could not keep track). I soon realized that I was a world class rabbit raiser! I could raise rabbits like no one's business. I visualized becoming the rabbit baron of the entire world. People would call me the 'rabbit man' or 'bunny master' and everyone who wanted a rabbit would have to come to me because I knew more about rabbits than anyone else in the world.

I had two cages that I moved my rabbits between in order to stop having bunnies. One cage was for moms and one for dads, which did not work very well because I did not know the difference. When a bundle of bunnies showed up in one pen, I knew I had a bad mix, so I would adjust and then magically, out of nowhere, another bunch of bunnies showed up in the other cage.

Another issue I had with my rabbits was that I had no idea what to do with them. They were not "eating" rabbits because they all had names. Even though everyone in my home town knew about me raising rabbits, no one was asking me about buying any.

Fortunately, I made a life changing decision to get a summer job, which effectively ended my rabbit raising career. I was lucky to find someone who wanted to buy all my rabbits. I did not charge anything for them because they all had names. I made it quite clear that my rabbits were not for eating. Unfortunately, not long after the transfer of all my friends, I found out that they were being housed in the guy's freezer. I should have known better than to give them to someone who fishes.

For the next couple of weeks, I had visions of flinging my trusty ole' Rope Saw up around one of those big bad limbs and then zip, zip, zip, crack, bang, and onto the next limb.

I went fishing and sat on the shore. At home I sat around on the patio and read books, watched action movies (not anything about chain saws or massacres). If I had had any idea what I was in for, I would have given Jed another call. It is funny how the dumbest ideas do not look particularly dumb. Looking back, trimming this huge tree with a Rope Saw was a dumb idea. It was also dangerous.

The Rope Saw holiday ended with the expected penultimate event; the Rope Saw arrived. I did not create the word penultimate. One of my bosses used the word. When he first did, I nodded my head like I understood. Later I looked it up. Since then, I have not had the opportunity to use the word much. It means the thing that happens just before the last thing happens, which was me using the Rope Saw.

I admit I was excited when the Rope Saw came. I tore the box open and lifted the black steel chain from the box. It felt sturdy like a quality piece of equipment. Connected to each end of the saw was a pristine yellow rope; the kind you pull water skiers with. Which made me think I should buy a boat and try water skiing. The problem with that idea is that I do not have anywhere to park a boat. However, the lack of boat parking is no reason to cancel a wild idea. I have a boat now. It is parked at the dealer's business; he is selling it for me on consignment.

Looking through the box I found the neatest part of the Rope Saw kit, the red weight. The red weight is a small cloth bag of sand. Well, I think it is filled with sand. It could be something else more scientifically suited to Rope Saw use like beans or something. I took the bag in my hand to feel its weight; it felt good. I knew this thing was made to throw and I could not wait to throw it.

I visualized throwing the weighted bag over the limb with the precision of a special force's sniper. I looked through the rest of the contents in the box, threw the directions aside, and decided it was time for treemageddon (yet another novel word!). I put on my best old work clothes and headed out to the tree with my Rope Saw. I had the place to myself for a couple of hours and could do almost anything wild I could think of.

I unwrapped the Rope Saw and attached the red bag weight to one of the lines. I then tried to throw the bag over a limb that was about twenty feet high. The bag went up about fifteen feet and returned to the ground with a thump. I continued to try throwing the bag over the limb until I was close to being spent. Throwing the bag over the branch appeared to be a definite "no go". Realizing that my technique was likely the problem, I tried swinging the bag like David swung his sling when he smacked Goliath. It is a good thing David was not using my red bag because I do not think he could have thrown it any better than me. I could not throw the bag accurately enough to go over the limb. The bag was just too awkward to throw.

I started to wonder why the retailer did not know the bag was hard to throw over a high branch. The ad did say "High Limb Rope Chainsaw". I did not look at the picture in the ad very closely. Under most circumstances I like to assume as much as I possibly can to save time. Unfortunately, it became obvious that I would have to read the instructions. I noticed that the picture on the instructions was of a branch that was over twenty feet high. But there was no way I could throw the bag that high. If the saw was made for cutting branches over twenty feet high, surely the retailer would have known average people cannot throw the bag that high. Then it occurred to me; it was a Professional High Limb Rope Saw! Only a professional would know the proper technique for throwing the bag over high limbs. I was just an amateur. I would need to learn how the professionals did it.

I tried throwing the bag again using the underhand method the same way you throw a bowling ball. But I never got close to getting the bag over the branch. I quickly came to realize that the weight was nice, but it did not work for me. I tried to fling the weight a few more times and was finally able to hit the crotch where the branch joined the tree. The bag landed in the crotch and just lay there. But the bag needed to travel completely through the crotch of the tree so I could pull the Rope Saw into place. I tried to wag the rope so the weight would fall through the crotch to the other side, which was a ridiculous idea that did not work.

I yanked the weight back down to the ground. After about a dozen more throws the weight went through the crotch and hung in the air on the opposite side of the limb. This was good. However, the weight was hanging a little too far off the ground for me to reach, so I needed to come up with a way to reach it.

It was a simple matter to reach the bag. I used a stepladder and a rake. It is the first of many methods that I devised and I used it many times while working with the Rope Saw. I call it the Stepladder Rake Maneuver (see Figure 18). I realize that some of the methods I defined were trivial, but the details about how I met each challenge were important lessons for me that contributed to the outcome of my adventure.

I mistakenly assumed that cutting branches with the Rope Saw would be simply placing the saw on the branch and then cutting it off. I found there was much more to it and that the number of challenges was overwhelming.

I looked forward to trying the Rope Saw for the first time, but I would soon not have the backyard to myself, since people were getting off work.

I was at a party with many friends once. When I got home, I found that I had some mustard on my cheek from eating something at the party. I thought it was odd that no one noticed it. I wrapped the Rope Saw Line around the tree in the most non-obvious way I could, and

hoped it would not draw any more attention than a glob of condiment.

The lessons I learned that day were valuable. I learned the Stepladder Rake Maneuver and that I would not need a membership at the health club. I would like to add that the Stepladder Rake Maneuver has taught me patience. I made many trips to the garage to get the stepladder and rake. It was a necessary part of the procedure. It would have been easy to become upset and inadvertently raise my blood pressure every time the weight hung up out of my reach, but it was not an issue since I expected it to happen.

The following day, having the place to myself again, I had a couple more hours to continue my mission. The leading saw rope line was threaded around the test branch. The next step was to pull the rope so that the Rope Saw was placed on the branch. I pulled the saw into place. After connecting the handholds to the saw, I gave it a pull to see how it felt and I felt nothing. I then realized that the saw had a cutting edge only on one side and that the non-cutting side was facing the branch. It was now necessary to somehow get the cutting side of the saw to face down against the branch.

To get the saw to roll over, I started to shake the rope lines, but that had no effect. I tried twisting the lines, but the saw would not roll over. Next, I pulled the Rope Saw off the branch and yanked it back onto the branch several times until the teeth were finally facing down.

While wildly flaying the Rope Saw Lines, I noticed a flat blade on one side of the saw. For the second time in as many days, I read the instructions and found that the flat blade is called a Flip Tab. The Flip Tab needed to be the first thing that went over the branch, ahead of the Rope Saw. The Flip Tab flips the Rope Saw over so the teeth of the Rope Saw face the branch (see Figure 21a). Sometimes it took a few tries to get the Flip Tab to flip the teeth down, but I found it did work well.

With the Rope Saw teeth facing down, I put the handholds onto the ropes (see Figure 21b). The hand holds are made of webbing. The saw is

19

pulled from side to side using the handholds. The proper way to hold the handholds was important; as I would soon understand why.

The Rope Saw came with twenty-five-foot lines attached to each side. If the branch was twenty-five feet above the ground, then I would have about six feet of slack when cutting a branch. The instructions say you should not stand under the limb being cut. For safety reasons, this made sense. I found it was necessary to add lengths of rope to the Rope Saw Lines so that I did not stand under a branch being cut.

The instructions were clear and I followed them. What I foolishly did, to begin with, was to stand under the branch while being ready to run when the branch began to fall. The branch made noise just before breaking off, which gave me time to bolt from under it before it fell. This was extremely dangerous for me to do, if I had stumbled or fallen, the branch could have hit and injured me. I only did it twice. After that, I added line to the Rope Saw Lines, so I did not have to stand under a branch.

What I ended up doing was using a Security Line to keep the branch from falling after it was cut. Instead of falling, the Security Line kept a cut branch hanging harmlessly in the air until I let it down using the Security Line. I always used extreme caution when using the Security Line because, although it never happened, the Security Line could have failed to stop a branch from falling. I always ensured the Rope Saw Lines were long enough so that I never stood under a branch I was cutting.

With some slack on the Rope Saw Lines, so I was not directly underneath the branch. I said directly, because the branch was long and I was standing just off to the side of it. Speaking of long branches, I found they always looked shorter before I cut them. This was kind of a good thing, because, if I knew how big some of the branches were before I cut them down, I would have been much more apprehensive.

With the saw teeth facing down, I grabbed the handholds. I knew, when I started to cut the limb, it would be one of those lifetime

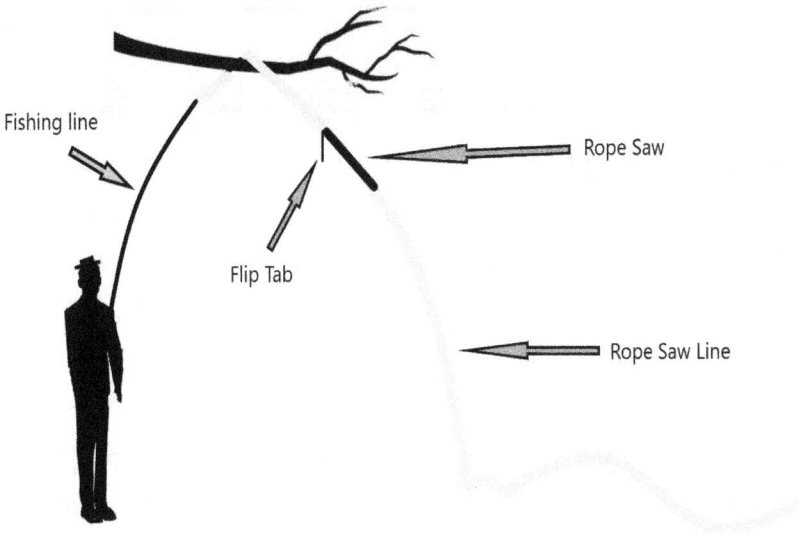

Fishing line

Rope Saw

Flip Tab

Rope Saw Line

Figure 21a

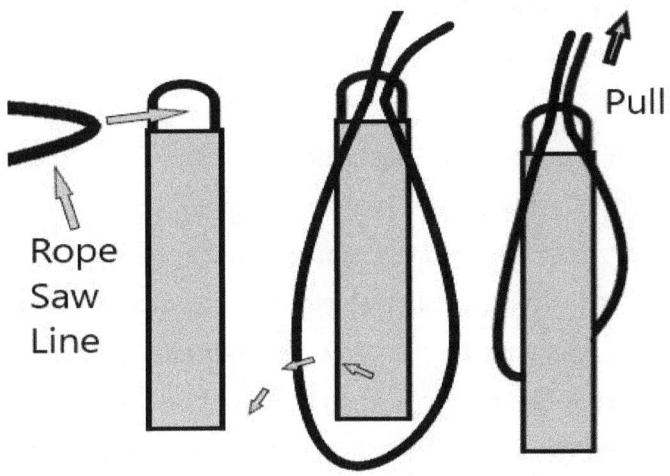

Rope Saw Line

Pull

Figure 21b

moments I would never forget. I knew if I did not run as soon as I heard the branch start breaking off, that it would really be an unforgettable experience. I took a deep breath and started pulling. To my astonishment, I saw wood shavings slowly fluttering down and landing around me. I realized the saw was really cutting the branch! With nervous excitement I continued pulling the saw; first with my left hand, and then with my right hand. Each time a mass of wood shavings fluttered out of the cut. Being new, the saw was cutting very well. As I pulled back and forth, I watched the channel make its way slowly to the bottom of the eight-inch-thick branch.

Because it was all new and entertaining to me, I did not pay attention to how many times I had to pull. Seldom have I had a wild idea work as well as this wild idea was. When there was only about a half an inch left to cut completely through the branch, I entered a heightened state of alertness because I would have to run when the branch fell to avoid being hit by it. I was aware that the instructions warned strongly against standing under a branch being cut and the last thing I wanted to do was prove anyone right. Besides, if the branch did get me, the first thing emergency personnel would do when they arrived, and found me pinned under the branch, would be to read the instructions.

I began to pull the Rope Saw back and forth again. Even though I was not standing directly under the branch, I was prepared to bolt away from the drop zone like a professional athlete ready for the one-hundred-yard dash. The cut looked so close to being all the way through the branch that I was amazed it had not broken off. I pulled ever more slowly, then there was a loud crack; so loud that anyone within a block of the tree would have heard it. I dropped the ropes and hightailed it to the garage where I stopped and looked back just in time to see the branch hit the ground, the small branches broke off like an explosion and scattered around the tree. I gave myself a high five and yelled an audible "Yes!", which anyone within a block of the tree would have heard too.

The branch was down. The Rope Saw worked just as I expected it to. I looked the branch over like a hunter inspecting a trophy buck. I was surprised to see all the small secondary branches laying around the yard. They were strewn farther from the tree than I would have expected.

The Rope Saw had fallen with the branch and the Rope Saw Lines were a tangle of ropes tightly knotted around the branch. The mess the branch made would need to be cleaned up before cutting any more branches since they would be a tripping hazard. I soon found that cleanup would be the easiest and the most stress-free part of using the Rope Saw.

3
Hitting the Mark

Whoever designed the Rope Saw had their ducks in a row. The Rope Saw is designed very well. I give much credit to the inventor. Coming up with the idea of taking the chain off a chain saw and attaching ropes to each end of the chain, so that it could be thrown over a branch and pulled by hand to cut a branch, was a top-of-the-line invention.

My first try at cutting a branch was successful, and I was ready to start removing the other branches that were threatening my garage, house, and billfold. In all, there were about five dead branches that fit the description.

I knew that using the Crawl Walk Run Method when trying something new and dangerous, like trimming the tree, would be the best way to continue. One of my old bosses introduced me to the concept. It was one of his great ideas and it has worked for me often. The Crawl Walk Run Method means, simply, to take it slow when starting a new and untested project. I am glad the method came to mind, and it proved helpful as I moved forward using the Rope Saw.

The second Target Branch was higher than the first branch I cut, but it was the lowest of all the remaining dead branches. My intention was to work my way up the tree. This made good sense. By removing the lower branches first, it would clear the way for throwing the bag to the next lowest branch.

I found that it would take a long time to become a talented bag thrower. It took me almost two hours of throwing to get the Rope Saw close to where I wanted to cut the next Target Branch. After that much throwing I needed a rest. While taking a break from throwing the bag, I conceived one of my best ideas ever.

It surprises me that the obvious is sometimes not easy to see. I have read all of Arthur Conan Doyles' *Sherlock Holmes* stories, so deduction is something I think I am pretty good at. I deduced that, since the bag was heavy and difficult to throw, using something other than the bag, which was not as heavy as the bag, made good sense.

Another idea that came to mind at the same time, was to use my archery bow. I could attach the string to a fishing arrow and then shoot the arrow over the branch. I am not the best at shooting a bow, but I can shoot it well enough to hit a paper plate at thirty yards. I had a thirty -pound target-recurve bow that would be perfect to use. Even though the bow was not immensely powerful, I knew the challenge would be to control how far the arrow flew.

While on a family visit several years ago, my brother in-law let me shoot his new compound bow. He lived in a large town and had a target set up in his backyard. At that time, new mechanical string releases were becoming popular, coincidentally, he had one of the new releases. I had never tried one of the releases and, since I was trying out his compound bow, he let me try out his mechanical release too.

As I Drew the bow string back using the mechanical release, I aimed the arrow into the sky. After the string was pulled completely back, I planned to lower my aim down, bringing it to point at the target. Once it was pointed at the target, I would let the arrow fly. Not being familiar with the mechanical release, as I raised the arrow skyward, I accidentally hit the release trigger on the release and let the arrow go. Like an F16 Fighter plane, it disappeared into the great blue. Only two words came to mind at that moment: not and good.

For the next hour we searched feverishly for the arrow. I was certain we would find someone lying in their yard with an arrow sticking in them. At the very least I thought we would find someone's brand new pickup truck with an arrow sticking in the roof. To my relief, we found the arrow sticking in a nearby yard. I did not give the bow any more tries. Remembering the experience, I realized using the bow to route a line was a bad idea.

However, using something lighter than the bag was a promising idea. I played tennis before buying a house with a big tree, so I had a collection of used tennis balls in the garage. I never threw old tennis balls away even though no one plays tennis with old balls because they do not bounce very well. I used the old balls for practice, and I liked to draw smiley faces on them and place them in various places around the garage for fun. Replacing the sandbag with a tennis ball was perfect.

I grabbed a tennis ball and poked a hole in it. I tied a knot at the end of the Rope Saw Line and pushed it into the tennis ball. Perfect. I then tried to throw the tennis ball overhanded across the Target Branch, but the tennis ball was not heavy enough to carry the weight of the rope, so the ball fell far short. I tried a few more times without good result, before I thought of using a lighter rope instead of the Rope Saw Line. If I could get a lighter line over the branch, I could splice it to the Rope Saw Line and use it to pull the Rope Saw Line over the branch.

The Rope Saw Line was a quarter inch thick. It was obvious that it was too heavy for the ball to carry it far. Looking around the garage for something that was lighter, I found braided fishing line. The fishing line was rated to carry sixty pounds, which would be strong enough to pull the Rope Saw Line over the branch.

To attach the fishing line to the tennis ball, I poked a hole in the ball all the way through the ball, then using a needle-nose pliers, stuck the fishing line through the ball and tied a knot in it so it would not slip back through the ball.

I stripped a good amount of fishing line off the spool, then tried throwing the ball overhand over the branch. The ball flew straight toward the branch. When it was within ten feet of it, it stopped abruptly and fell to the ground because I was standing on the string. I carefully rearranged the fishing line, being careful not to stand on it, and gave it another throw. The ball got within a couple of feet of the branch and then stopped abruptly again. I needed to strip more line off the spool. With sufficient line laying on the ground I tried again. The ball flew toward the target, ricocheted off a nearby branch and fell to the ground. It was clear that the tennis ball was going to work much better than the bag.

I continued trying to throw the ball over the branch. After a while, I realized the overhand method was not working well for me. It would be a different matter if I had the arm of a professional baseball pitcher. Of course, I do not. If I did, I would be playing professional baseball for a big -league team, rolling in the bucks, and calling a professional tree trimmer to take care of the tree.

After experimenting, I found that throwing the ball, the way David from the Bible swung his slingshot, was easier on my arm. By twirling the ball in a circle and letting it go at the precise time, it was easier, and I could make the ball go much farther. Things were coming together for a workable method to use the Rope Saw.

David's Slingshot Method worked well, except that the accuracy was not good. I could not throw the ball with the same precision that David shot his slingshot. I thought my accuracy would improve with practice.

The accuracy of my bow and arrow idea came to mind again, but then my brother-in-law's compound bow incident came to mind as well.

As I gained more experience throwing the tennis ball, my accuracy did improve. But it was still taking too many throws to get close to the target. Eventually, and after a countless number of tries, I was able to throw the tennis ball over the Target Branch.

I found that, if a throw were good, the fishing line would feed freely to the ball and the line would travel over the branch, string would continue to feed to the ball, and it would end up on the ground. Sometimes the line would hang up in the tree with the ball hanging in the air. By shaking the line, to feed line to the ball, it would most often allow the ball to fall to the ground. There were times when no amount of shaking would free the line. If the ball were hanging within reach, I would use the Stepladder Rake Maneuver (see figure 18).

I mentioned that my backyard has a privacy fence. I am thankful that it does because we all know that the common public can be cruel, insensitive, and laugh at you uncontrollably under certain circumstances. I experiment with wild ideas in the backyard. The funny thing is, I trimmed trees for years in the backyard before I realized the neighbors and motorists, driving on the street in front of my house, could see much of what I was up to. The tree was much higher than my house so they could not see me. But they could see the ropes, the balls flying, and the sawing activity if they were paying attention. I hope they were not paying attention.

My next door neighbors have a little dog. The dog liked to watch the backyard through their patio door. The little canine never failed to notice when I had a wild throw that sent one of my tennis balls into her backyard. I am sure she loved to play fetch like all dogs, and being stuck in the house, when she saw the ball come bouncing in her backyard, she went crazy barking and barking. I am thinking the neighbor lady probably went a little crazy about the whole deal too.

Since the ball had a string attached to it, with the opposite end of the string attached to me, I would as quickly as possible, pull the ball back over the fence into my yard. This really excited the dog because dogs know a magical tennis ball when they see one. My neighbor was likely not as observant and did not see the ball.

At the time I used black fishing line, which is invisible unless you know it is attached to the ball. If she had seen the ball flying into their yard, she would have been as amazed as her little dog to see the ball magically fly out of the yard. It could only be imagined what the dog was thinking; "Did you see that? Did you? It's been going on for days... it's driving me crazy!" And the neighbor lady would likely have said: "Yeah! I see it!"

Throwing the ball to a branch was complicated if there were leaves in the way. There was some wisdom in trimming trees in the spring before they leafed out. The problem with waiting was that it was sometimes more difficult to tell which branches were dead if they did not have a chance to leaf out first. I did not want to remove any live branches.

Leaves would divert the tennis ball from hitting the Target Branch. Sometimes the fishing string would become tangled in the leaves or small branches. When that happened, I would try to pull the tennis ball free or try to feed it more string by whipping the string so the ball would fall to the ground.

When I was not able to untangle the fishing line, I would pull the fishing line until it broke from the tennis ball. Often, after the fishing line broke, the tennis ball would fall to the ground. There were more than a few times that the tennis ball remained tangled in the tree because the string did not break where it was attached to the ball, but instead, would break where the tangle was. During my tree trimming years, there were times when there were several tennis balls dangling in the tree. Fortunately, they were not any more obvious than a glob of condiment.

If the tennis ball were not in the correct place on the branch, and I could not pull it back off the branch because it would get tangled in leaves or small branches, I would feed the fishing line to the ball so that it would fall back to the ground. I would then cut the line from the tennis ball, pull the string back to the ground, and then reattach it to the tennis ball so I could give it another try. Cutting the tennis ball from the fishing line made it possible to pull the string over the branch through any tangles and back down to the ground.

Disconnecting the fishing string from the tennis ball to untangle the line, became so common that I devised an uncomplicated way to reattach the string to the tennis ball quickly. I pushed the point of a needle-nose pliers all the way through the tennis ball (see Figure 32a), then I grabbed the string with the end of the needle-nose and pulled it through the tennis ball. I added a large knot on the end of the fishing line (see Figure 32b) so that the string could not be pulled easily through the tennis ball. Later I found it necessary to tie the fishing line around the ball instead of relying on a knot to keep the fishing line attached to the ball.

By being careful to make the knot in the fishing line just the right size, the string would stay attached to the ball. However, if the ball became tangled in the tree, the knot could be forcibly pulled through the tennis ball. This made it a little easier to deal with tangles since it was not necessary to break the string. If a throw were perfect, the fishing line would be on the branch where the cut was going to be made, and the tennis ball would be on the ground (see Figure 36).

If the tennis ball was not placed on a branch exactly where a cut was to be made, and there were no obstacles that would stop the line from being moved to the exact position, then I would try to jiggle or whip the line to move it to the correct cutting position. If there was an obstacle that made it impossible to jiggle the line into position, then I cut the ball from the fishing string, pulled the fishing line back to the ground, retied

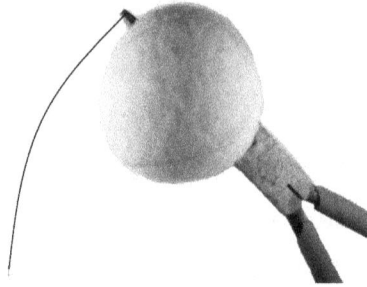

Figure 32a

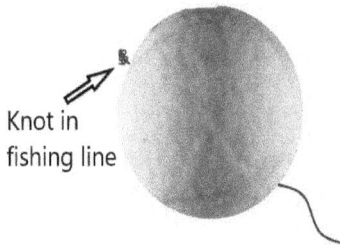

Knot in
fishing line

Figure 32b

it to the ball, and retried throwing the ball .

If the fishing line was in the correct cutting position, or if it could be moved to the cutting position by jiggling or whipping it, the fishing string was disconnected from the tennis ball and spliced to the Rope Saw Line (see figure 33a). The Rope Saw Line was then pulled across the branch using the fishing line (see Figure 33b).

Using the fishing line to pull the Rope Saw Lines over branches worked if the Rope Saw Lines were not too heavy. For higher branches, I had to add length to the Rope Saw Lines which added weight. At times, the fishing line could not handle the weight, so I spliced the fishing line to heavier nylon string, pulled the nylon string over the branch using the fishing line, and then spliced the nylon string to the Rope Saw Line to

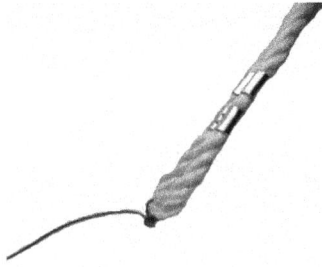

Figure 33a

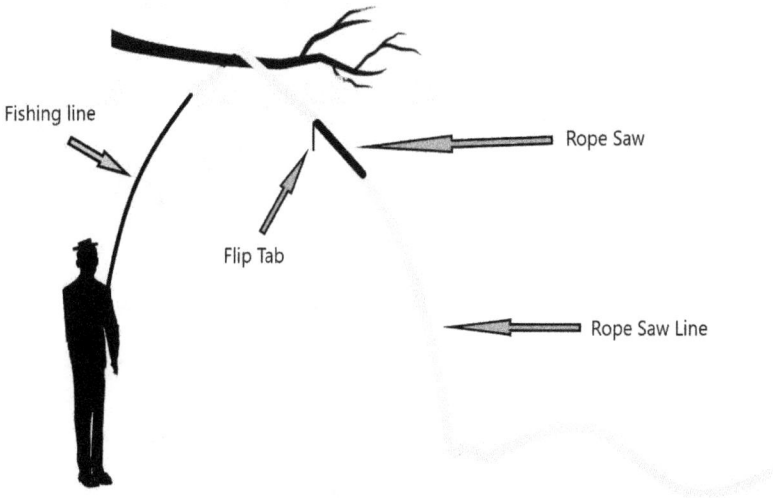

Figure 33b

Figure 33c

Figure 34a

Figure 34b

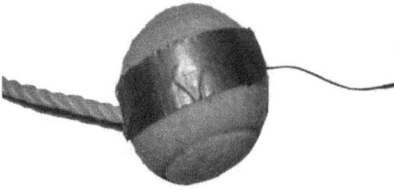

Figure 34c

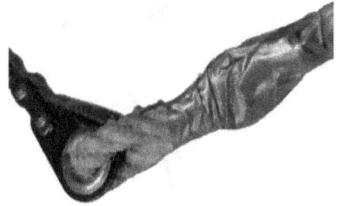

Figure 34d

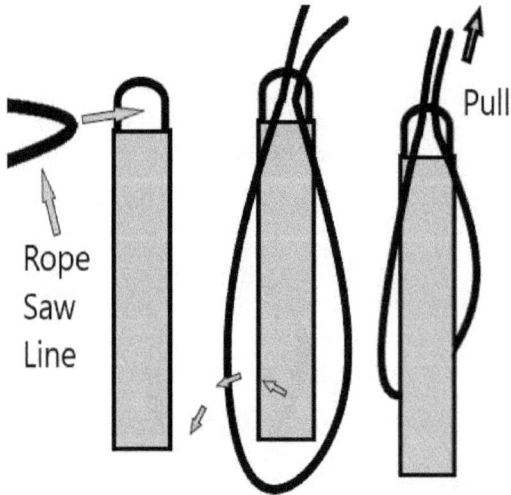

Rope
Saw
Line

Pull

Figure 34e

pull it over. Sometimes while threading the Rope Saw Line over a branch, the spliced lines would snag. To resolve this issue, I made a slit in a tennis ball on one side of the ball from top to bottom (see Figure 33c).

After splicing the Rope Saw Line to the fishing line (see Figure 34a). I inserted the splice inside the tennis ball (see Figure 34b) and then sealed the knot inside the tennis ball with duct tape (see Figure 34c). I also wrapped the Rope Saw Line connection with duct tape (see Figure 34d). This made it easier to slide the Rope Saw over the Target Branch.

At times getting the splice over a branch required extra force. A useful technique was to pull the tennis ball, with the splice in it, close to the branch, then give it a quick pull to bounce the ball on the branch. As the ball bounced up from the branch, I would yank it quickly across the branch.

The following figures are a review of the steps that I used to route the Rope Saw over a branch. The Rope Saw Line is routed in two steps – more than two if I needed to use increased strengths of lines. The first step was to route the fishing line (see Figure 36). If the fishing line was not strong enough to pull the Rope Saw Line over the branch, then the fishing line was spliced to a stronger line and the heavier line was pulled over the branch using the fishing line. The heavier line was then spliced to the Rope Saw Line and it was used to pull the Rope Saw Line (see Figure 37) over the branch. The result is shown in Figure 38.

With the Rope Saw placed at the exact location on the branch where I wanted to cut it. I was ready to begin cutting. I attached the handholds to the Rope Saw Lines (see Figure 34e).

The directions that came with the Rope Saw show the proper angle of a cut (see Figure 40). Immediately before reading the instructions about the angle of the cut, I found that the angle of the cut is important. As a cut travels through a branch, the branch can start pinching the saw. If the angle is incorrect, the branch can pinch the saw enough to freeze the saw in place in the branch. A saw can quickly become so stuck in a branch that it cannot be easily removed, at times, it became so stuck that I could not remove it. Anyone who is experienced with using a chain saw is good at not getting the saw stuck in a cut. Although I followed the instructions, the saw still stuck at times; which was clearly due to my inexperience.

With the handholds connected, I grasped the straps and gave it a nice easy pull. The saw moved smoothly across the branch and I noticed that there was not any sawdust falling. It was obvious that the teeth of the saw were not facing down against the branch. I was a little surprised

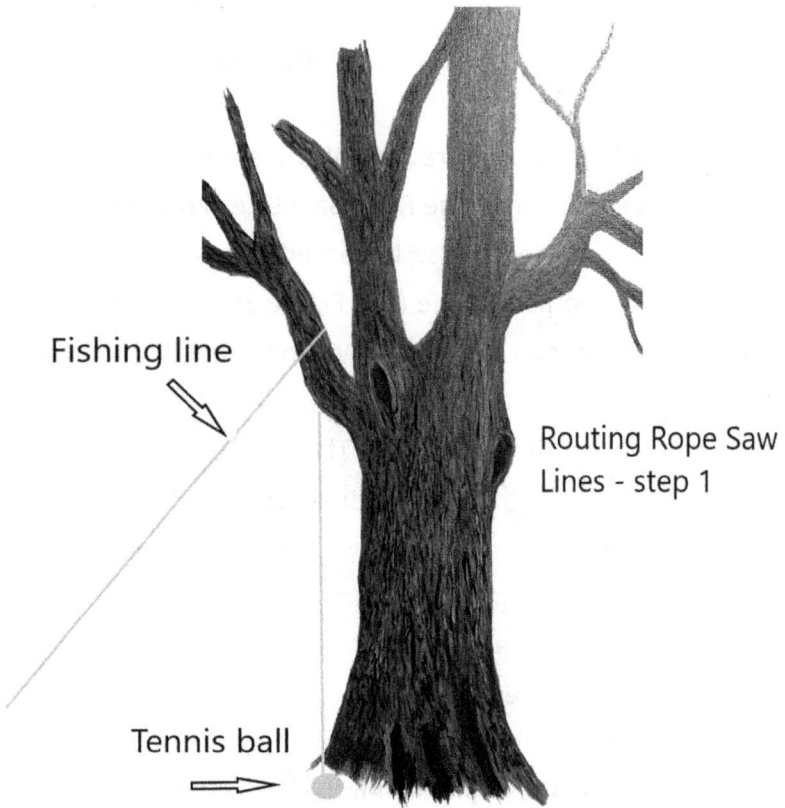

Fishing line

Routing Rope Saw
Lines - step 1

Tennis ball

Figure 36

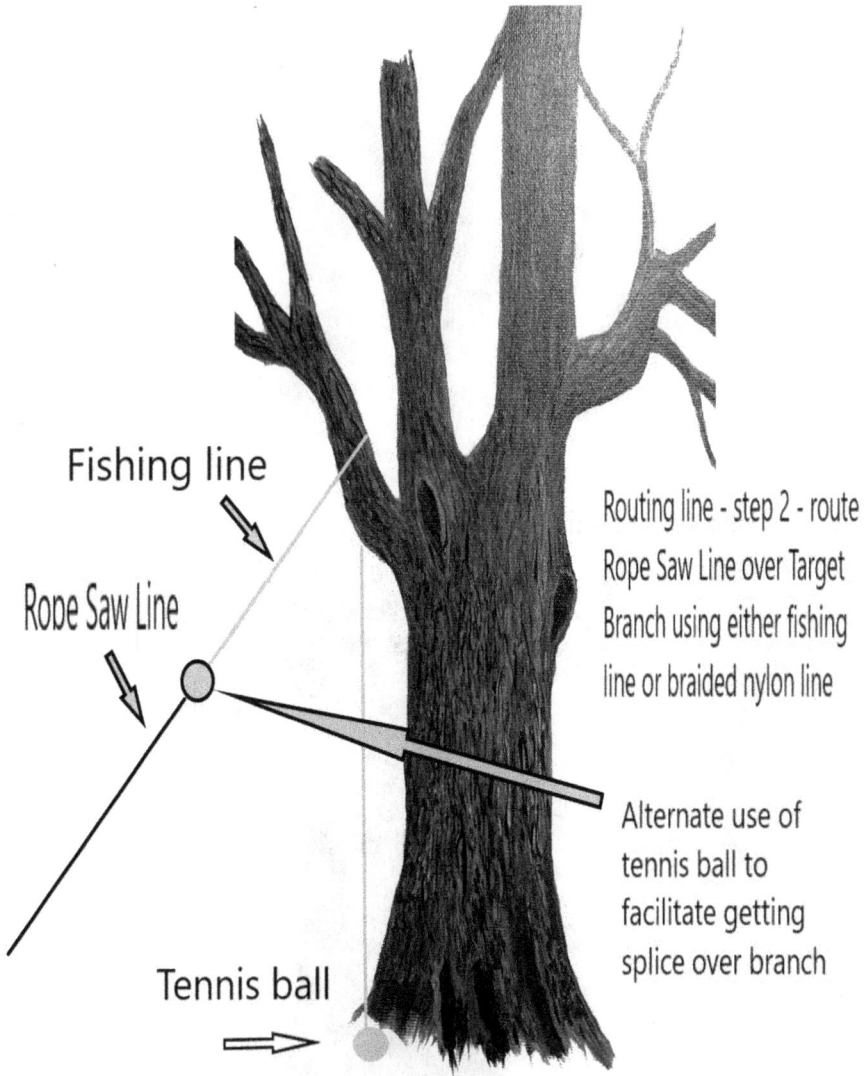

Fishing line

Rope Saw Line

Routing line - step 2 - route Rope Saw Line over Target Branch using either fishing line or braided nylon line

Alternate use of tennis ball to facilitate getting splice over branch

Tennis ball

Figure 37

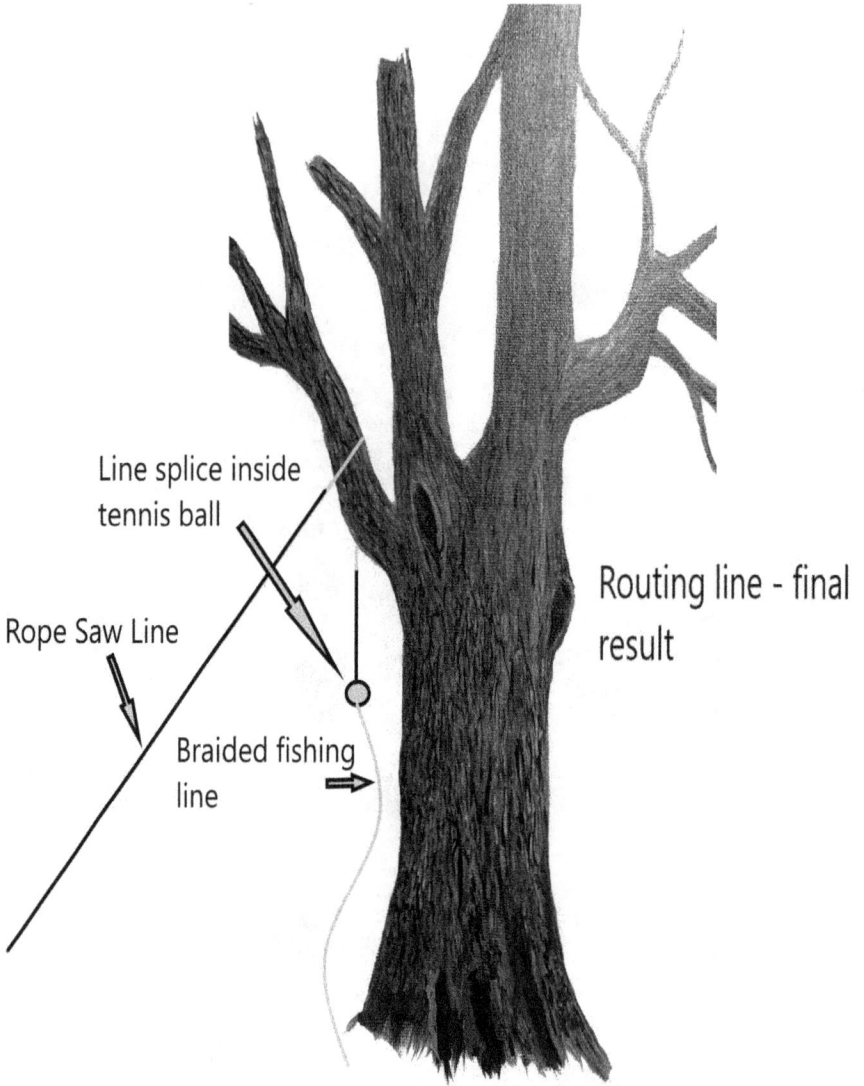

Figure 38

because the Flip Tab had crossed the branch when I pulled the saw onto it, but it obviously did not do its job. I found that the Flip Tab failed sometimes for whatever reason. I first confirmed that the teeth were not facing down by checking the Rope Saw with binoculars. I found that binoculars were useful for getting a close-up view of what was happening with the Rope Saw.

If the saw teeth were not facing down, they could be flipped by pulling the saw off the branch so that the Flip Tab could be pulled across the branch again. By doing this, I was usually able to get the saw to flip over.

It needs to be noted that once I started a cut, it was difficult to adjust anything. After a cut was started, sliding the saw out of the cut was impossible; it had to be lifted out of the cut.

I always made a point to double check everything closely before starting a cut. It was important that the saw was placed so that it was cutting straight through a branch. If the saw was sawing at a different angle on each side of the branch, the cut would take much longer and would be difficult to complete. Different angles on each side of a branch resulted in a "spiral" cut (see Figure 41). The saw had to cut straight through the branch. A spiral cut could make a saw stick tightly in the cut. Before a cut was made too deep to slide the saw from the cut, the cut had to be examined to ensure it was not a spiral cut. I made it a practice to inspect a cut after the first two pulls of the saw.

Once the saw teeth were facing the branch, the saw began to cut. As I pulled the saw alternately left then right, I could see the sawdust falling from the cut as expected.

Because the branch was so far up in the tree, I found I needed to add extra lengths to each of the Rope Saw Lines. When doing so, I needed to tie the knots as unobtrusively as possible so that they did not hang up when pulling them across a branch. I would also wrap the knots with duct tape so they would not snag anything (see Figure 34d). At times it

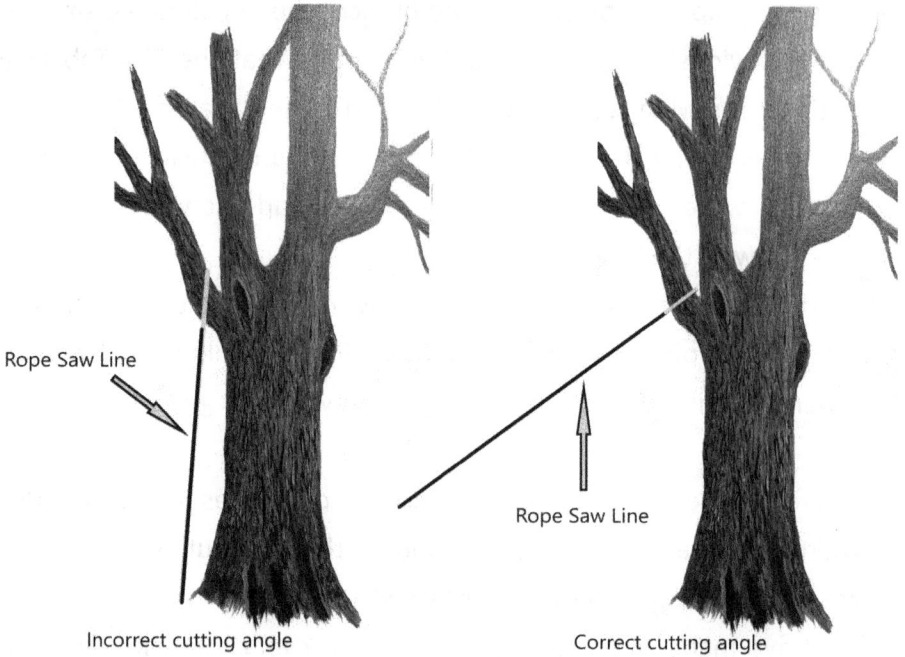

Rope Saw Line

Rope Saw Line

Incorrect cutting angle

Correct cutting angle

Figure 40

was necessary to insert the knots inside tennis balls to get them to go over a branch. By adding extra length to the Rope Saw Lines I was able to cut limbs as high as sixty feet and not stand under them.

The extra length of the Rope Saw Lines also made it possible for me to cut at the best angle while not standing directly under the branch. I was still careful to prepare myself to bolt when the branch started falling to the ground since there were secondary branches that would break and fall.

Cutting the second branch went forward without a hitch. I had to cut it completely through, as I did the first branch, before it fell to the ground. As with the first branch, it was like a bomb going off when it landed.

Just before a branch breaks, the sound of the wood cracking is heard. Jed, the tree expert, told me the type of tree I have was a White Poplar. Others have told me it was a Cottonwood. It really did not make any difference to me what it was. I knew it was one tough tree because branches never fell until they were cut completely through, and when the branch finally broke, the noise of it breaking was loud enough to be heard blocks away.

With the branch laying on the ground, I realized again how difficult it was to estimate the size of a branch while it was in the tree. I thought the branch was probably six feet long and fairly insignificant as far as weight. However, once on the ground, I found the branch was at least three times longer and weighed close to eighty pounds. I made a mental note of how easy it was to underestimate the size and weight of a branch. It was obvious that the damage a branch can do was related to the length and weight of the branch.

The branch being safely on the ground, I used my twelve-inch electric chain saw to finish the job. After trimming the small branches off the limb and cutting them into fireplace-size logs, I piled them neatly in preparation for the coming winter. The small branches were tied up to await transport to the dump. Having completed my first official tree

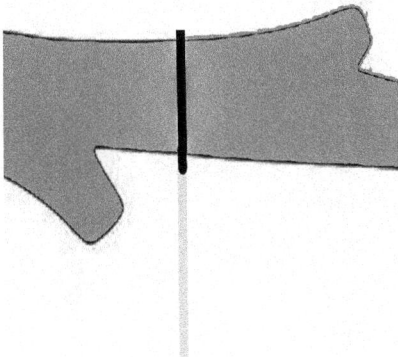

Correct angle. Saw is at a ninety degree angle on each side of the branch

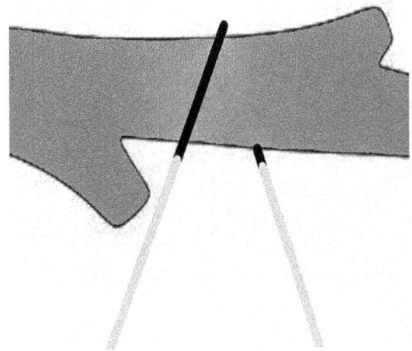

Incorrect angle. Saw is cutting a different angle on each side of the branch

Figure 41

trimming operation, I was ready to head to the big time.

4
The Lacking Lumberjack

Armed with my experience, I spent my free time cutting branches off Moby Tree; a name I gave the tree that was well earned. I had my procedure down, all the equipment I needed, and plenty of branches to trim. My plan was simple. I was going to take the easy branches first and then move on to the ones that were not so easy. The only challenge was that I had no idea which ones were easy and which ones were not. I admit, at this point in my tree trimming experience, I was having a little fun. But it was just a little.

The next branch I attacked was ten inches in diameter. Of course this was an estimate. I found that throwing the tennis ball was one of the most time-consuming parts. I never hit any branch the first time and it often took hours to get the ball where I wanted it. On many occasions the ball would just get close. I would then have to pull the fishing line back off the branch and start over. Of all the tasks related to tree trimming, I think throwing the ball was the most fun and the most aggravating.

There was one time that it took hours to get the fishing string over a branch in the place I wanted it. After finally hitting the right spot, and to this day I am not sure if I saw what I thought I saw, but I would swear a squirrel ran to the line and cut it with his teeth before my very eyes. I was speechless. Was the squirrel trying to protect the tree?

After an hour or so, I was able to route the fishing line over the branch near where it needed to be. I disconnected the tennis ball, connected the fishing line to the Rope Saw Line, and sealed it inside the tennis ball. I pulled the Rope Saw Line over the branch and made sure the teeth of the saw were facing the branch. I connected the handholds and double checked everything. It was going to be an easy cut. I was a little concerned about the branch being a little big, but I looked it over good and decided that it would fall straight down without hurting anything. I did put boards on a stone wall, that I thought the branch might hit, just in case the branch had enough weight to hurt the stone wall.

The earlier cut, being about an eight-inch branch, took much work to cut. Still, the Rope Saw was new, and so it cut through the branch quickly. I noticed that the eight-inch branch took more energy than the test cut I made, but I attributed that to the thickness of the branch. The handholds, which are made of thick webbing, were a little hard on the hands. The longer I had to cut, the more I noticed the discomfort. Snaking my hands through the webbing, so that the force of the pull was focused on my wrists, was more comfortable. I did not know at the time, but cutting a ten-inch branch was going to take some work.

I started to pull the saw back and forth and noticed sawdust coming from the limb. After about fifteen minutes of pulling, my arms were getting tired so I stopped to take a break. After several minutes, and after checking the cut with my binoculars, I was ready to start cutting again. After another fifteen minutes I needed another break. I started wondering if the saw had become dull because of the first two cuts, but it did not seem likely to me. While cutting up the first two limbs with my electric chain saw, I noticed that the wood was very dense and tough. With that in mind, I thought the wood was so dense and tough that it prematurely dulled the blade. But the Rope Saw was still cutting because sawdust continued to fall from the cut. The Rope Saw was working fine, it just took time to cut through the branch; especially one that was ten inches thick.

After the third break, my arms were very tired. I reduced my Rope Saw "pull" time to less than five minutes between breaks. I was not disappointed that the cutting was taking so long, I knew the wood was dense and I expected it to take a long time.

After forty minutes of cutting, I could see that the saw had nearly cut completely through the branch. As I mentioned, I was always amazed that the saw had to cut completely through a branch before the branch broke off. With my binoculars I could see there was only a half inch of the branch left to cut. Yet the branch would not break off the tree by virtue of its weight.

Being very tired from all the pulling, and being in somewhat of a quandary because the branch was not breaking off when I expected, I was unknowingly in for a real surprise. As mentioned earlier, I was holding the Rope Saw handholds by wrapping the straps around my wrists and holding them so the pulling force was focused on my wrists. I prepared to bolt when the branch broke. I knew that it would be a complete surprise, so I was a little on edge. As with the other branches, I was not directly under the branch, and I was standing far enough from the tree so that only a small portion of the branch was barely above me. I figured when the branch broke, the part of the branch closest to the tree would fall straight down last, and the part of the branch farthest from the tree would fall down first, angling itself closer to the tree, giving me more time to flee the strike area. What I did not consider was that I had entrapped my hands in the handholds. My hands were entwined in the handholds and, when the branch broke, it fell on the Rope Saw Lines. The branch, easily weighing over one hundred pounds, began pushing the Rope Saw Lines to the ground while pulling me toward the tree and under the falling branch. Realizing what was happening, I was barely able to free my hands from the straps and run from the falling branch before it crashed to the ground. It was a remarkably narrow escape, especially because the branch was a very heavy one; so heavy I could not lift it.

The first thing I did was to check if anyone saw my close call. Gladly, I was saved again from any embarrassment by the privacy of my backyard. This was a lesson I have not forgotten. The weight of the branch, pulling me under it and crushing me beneath it, would have effectively put an end to my tree trimming. Providence came through for me again.

While cutting branches it is easy to get tired and sloppy about safety. As I learned how to use the Rope Saw, I found the best policy is to take my time. There were multiple things to think about when cutting a branch. I had to always be aware of the impending dangers. How I held the Rope Saw handholds was particularly important. I was very blessed to learn how not to hold the straps (see Figure 48a) before I was injured. The correct way (see Figure 48b) allowed me to quickly release the straps. I overlooked this simple issue once. I never did it again.

The directions warned that I should not stand directly under a branch when cutting it. Where I stood depended on how long the Rope Saw Lines were. They had to be long enough so that I was not forced to stand under a branch during the cut. Adding length to the Rope Saw Lines also allowed me to cut at the proper angle. For added safety, I used a Security Line to keep the branch suspended in the air after it was cut.

The length of the Rope Saw Lines also helped to get a saw unstuck. If the lines were long enough, I could move my position more easily. By moving my position, and snapping the Rope Saw Lines, I could sometimes free the saw. The extra length also helped avoid pulling the saw too tightly while cutting, allowing me to let the saw rest in the cut without putting force on it, which prevented the saw from getting stuck.

They say when you get bucked off a horse, you need to get right back on the horse. So, I moved right onto the next branch after my heart stopped pounding from the near miss.

I ran track and cross-country when I was in high school. I am the first to say I was not good at it. I once ran a cross-country meet where I came in something like two hundred and seventh out of two hundred

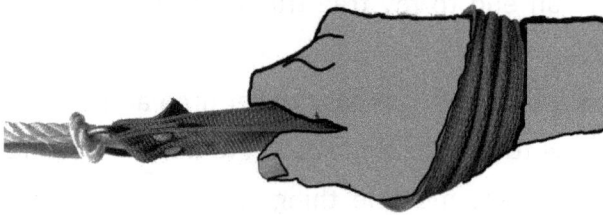

Figure 48a
WRONG way to hold handholds

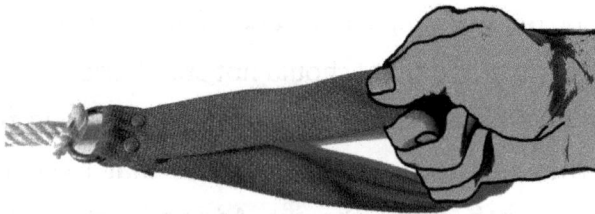

Figure 48b
CORRECT way to hold handholds

and eight contestants. I would have been last, except I bolted at the very last and beat the guy in front of me. It had to be a complete surprise to the guy or else I never would have been able to beat him. Honestly, we were running on grass, so I do not think he heard me coming up behind him. I will never forget my best friend laughing when I made that final dash. Looking back, coming in two hundred and seventh is not better than coming in two hundred and eight.

It is funny how things turn out though. Later in life I became good at distance running and was unusually fast for short distances. I never really understood why I came to enjoy running. I stopped running several years ago. The only time I want to run now is when a branch I am cutting is about to break. This story has nothing to do with me using a Rope Saw, but just in case the guy I beat that day is reading this, I wanted to apologize for sneaking up on him like that.

This picture, from the front cover, is the tree before I started trimming branches from it. If you look closely, you can see one of my wild ideas, which was to attach a saw to a long pole so I could cut a branch. The large branch, shooting to the right, broke off during a windstorm. When it broke, it smashed all but the bottom three feet of a fifteen-foot cherry tree, and thereby saved a fence from being damaged. The large branch breaking off alerted me to the damage a falling branch could cause and officially kicked off my tree trimming adventure.

Left. Having thrown the fishing line over the Target Branch, and then splicing it to a thicker rope, it was ready to be pulled across the branch.

Below. I used different thicknesses of ropes to route lines. I enclosed the splices in tennis balls to help get them over branches without snagging.

Right. The Carabiner Safety Line is connected in case the carabiner needs to be pulled back. Pulling the tennis ball caused the carabiner to travel up the rope and form a hangman's knot. The end opposite the knot was threaded over a Utility Branch to keep the branch from dropping to the ground after it is cut.

Preserving a good Security Branch (the highest forked branch in the photo) was beneficial. I used it to suspend all branches lower than it. In the photo, the line farthest to the right is the Carabiner Safety Line. The Security Line running from the forked Security Branch is tied to the Target Branch to keep it from falling to the ground and is anchored by being wrapped around the tree trunk. The center two lines are the Rope Saw Lines (one of the lines is difficult to see). They were pulled out of the way while the other lines were being routed. Everything is in place and ready for the cut.

Right: Ready to cut.

Bottom Right: This branch weighed over one hundred pounds and took an hour to cut.

Below: I held the handholds in a such a way so that I could release them instant-ly when the branch began to fall.

Above: Ready to cut

Left: Security line with branch suspended.

Below: My Rope Saw tools

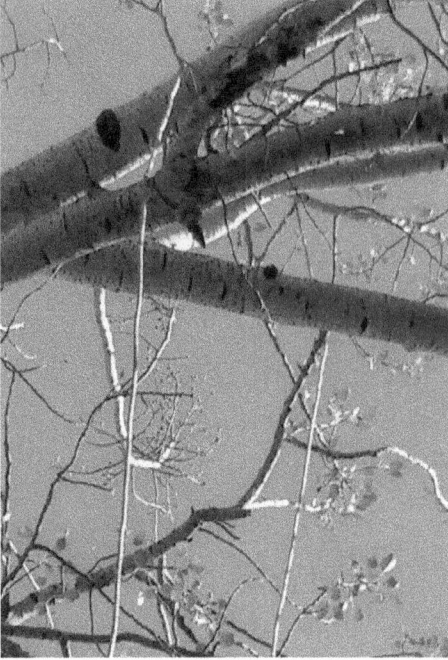

Left: Some branches were difficult to isolate. They required unusually accurate slingshot shots.

Right; Branch hanging safely after being cut.

My tree trimming adventure with Moby Tree comes to an end. The remaining trunk resembled a man raising his arms to the sky in total surrender.

This cut resulted in a spiral cut and an irretrievable Rope Saw. The cut was too close to the crotch of the tree and caused one side of the saw to cut at an angle different from the other side. After I bought a new saw, I made a cut above the stuck Rope Saw to remove the branch. A hard learned lesson and an easy mistake to make. I made it a habit to check a cut after the first two pulls of the Rope Saw to ensure it was cutting at the same angle on both sides of the branch.

When everything went right, the line was routed over the branch where I wanted to make a cut. The golf ball would travel completely through the tree branches and would land on the ground or would hang where I could reach it and pull it to the ground. If things did not go right, the line became tangled in the tree, and I had to break the line and hope the ball fell to the ground. The string was then pulled to the ground for another try.

Shooting a line into a tree with leaves and small branches made hitting the Target Branch, where the cut would be, much harder. Using the slingshot was more accurate than lobbing the tennis or golf ball.

Reminiscent of the cover photo

Upper Left: The crane did the heavy lifting. Upper Right: A branch is lifted away from the tree. Bottom: Removing the final branch.

5
Bombs Away

The branches that I had cut from the tree so far were Free Fall Branches. They were branches that would fall to the ground without hitting anything important like my garage, the house, the awning, the fence, or the neighbor's house. Any branches that would damage something I called Bomb Branches.

Cutting Bomb Branches was more dangerous because of how much they weighed. I knew without a foolproof method to avoid damaging anything, something would get bombed and it would not be pretty.

It was not immediately obvious how to protect structures from Bomb Branches. The Bomb Branches somehow needed to be stopped from falling on structures. There was no other way to protect anything from being damaged by a Bomb Branch.

I considered tying a rope around the Target Branch, then, when the branch began to fall, I would pull it away from damaging anything. The idea would require me to instantly grab and pull the Bomb Branch, while at the same time, running to avoid being hit by falling branches.

Bolting away from a falling branch was the most stressful time when cutting a branch. If I had to grab the security rope and use it to guide the branch down at the same time, the stress would be over the top; especially when the house or garage depended on my success. It was also doubtful that I would have enough strength to pull the heavy branches at all.

I logically surmised that it was too risky to assume that I could react fast enough to pull the branch away from falling on anything. Besides, if anything were to go terribly wrong, it would be when a cut was completing, and the branch was beginning to fall to the ground. For that reason, I did not want to add the complexity to the moment, which was reason enough to trash the whole idea.

Another problem with the idea was that I could not give the idea a test run, since a bad run would result in a large hole in the roof of my house. It seemed the only way to stop a Target Branch from damaging anything was to keep it from falling by tying it to something. It was obvious that a higher branch would work best. If the Target Branch could be tied to a higher branch, the only remaining challenge was how to do it.

A separate rope would need to be used. The easy part about using another rope was that the placement of the rope was not as important as placing the Rope Saw. It just had to be in a location on the Target Branch where it was strong enough to keep the Target Branch from falling. It then had to be routed over an equally strong branch that could hold the weight of the Target Branch.

I liked the idea, but I was not happy about routing another line using the Tennis Ball Method. Using another rope could add hours of extra work to each branch cutting. What made the other rope worthwhile, was that in addition to protecting any threatened structures from being damaged; it would also protect me. The Security Line, which is what I named it, would afford me one more level of protection from falling branches. I would still need to use caution, but the odds were much less likely that any branches would fall on me.

The first thing I did was throw a one-fourth-inch polypropylene rope over the Target Branch (see Figure 66a). It was not critical where the Security Line was placed on the Target Branch, it just had to be placed so the Security Line would hold the weight of the Target Branch, without the Target Branch breaking where the line was placed. It was much easier to throw the Security Line over the Target Branch because the placement was not as important as placing the Rope Saw.

Then I attached a carabiner to the security rope (see Figure 66b). I preferred using the quick link carabiners (see Figure 67a), rather than the clip carabiner (see Figure 67b), because the clip carabiner could accidentally open and cause an injury or damage something. Being able to lock the carabiner was the best choice even if it took longer to do.

A friend of mine talked me into going rock climbing once. I cannot explain why I decided to go; as I have said, I do not like heights. Maybe I was not associating rock climbing with heights. Anyway, the first rock we decided to climb was about one hundred feet high. Thankfully, my inability to estimate heights was at work and the rock did not look all that high to me. I thought it was doable; whatever that means. My friend was well versed in rock climbing and would not take any rock-climbing shortcuts at all. He went straight by the book, and I liked that. He first showed me how to connect the ropes and how to communicate correctly with the person holding the safety rope, who I keenly realized was an especially important person. After the training session, he ascended the rock and connected the safety line to a connecting point that he had hammered into the rock near the top. He descended and then it was my turn.

I got all harnessed up, connected to the Security Line and started to ascend. I made it up to about six feet off the ground and was doing very

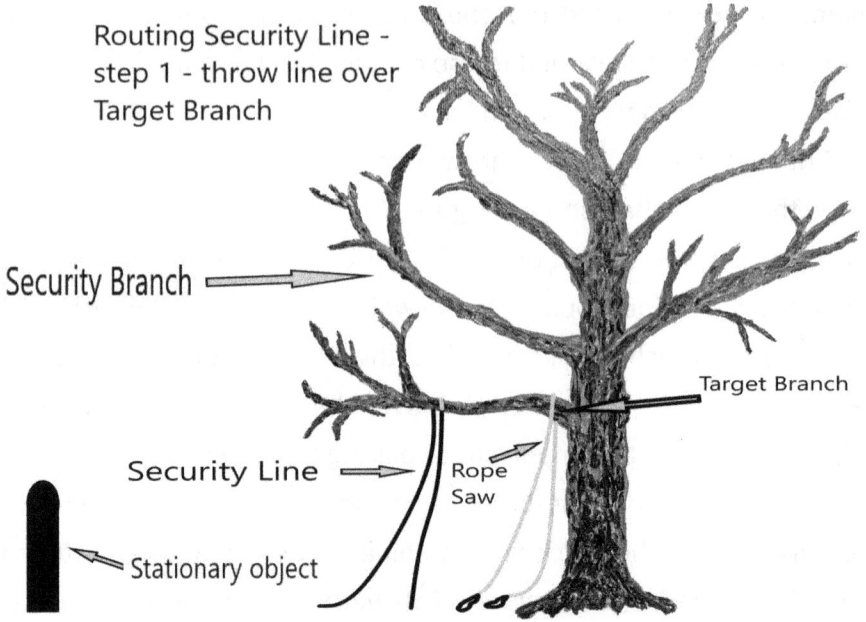

Routing Security Line -
step 1 - throw line over
Target Branch

Security Branch

Target Branch

Security Line

Rope
Saw

Stationary object

Figure 66a

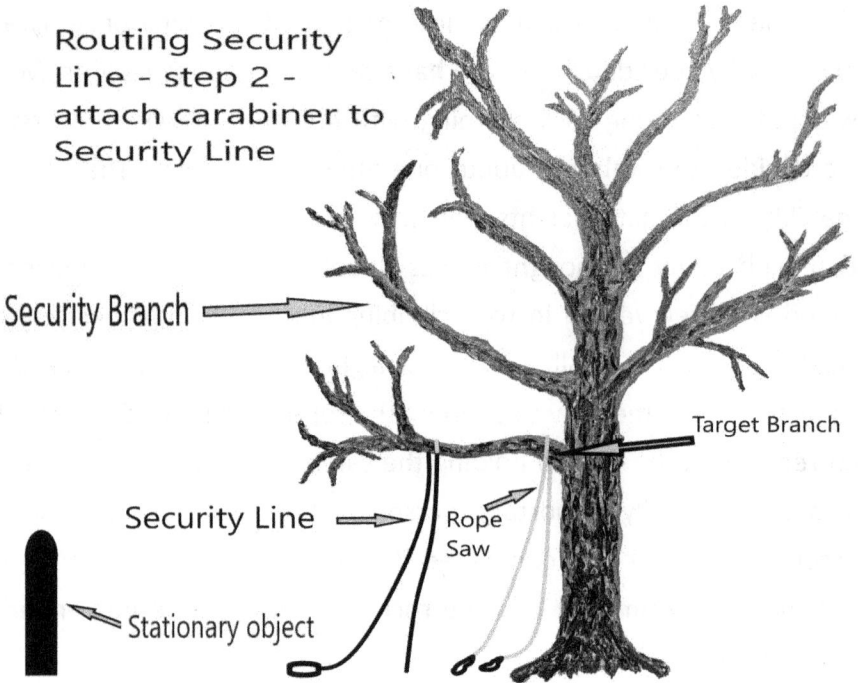

Routing Security
Line - step 2 -
attach carabiner to
Security Line

Security Branch

Target Branch

Security Line

Rope
Saw

Stationary object

Figure 66b

Carabiner

Figure 67a

Figure 67b

Routing Security Line - step 3 - attaching Carabiner Safety Line to carabiner

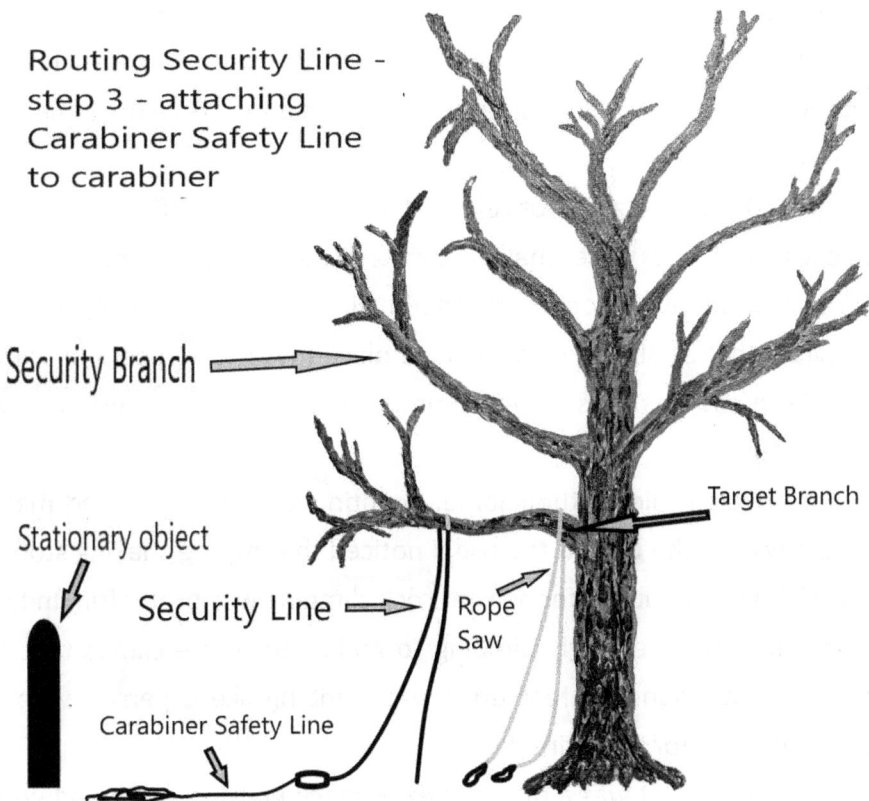

Security Branch

Target Branch

Stationary object

Security Line

Rope Saw

Carabiner Safety Line

Figure 67c

67

well. I could visualize ascending Mount McKinley at this point, but only if Mount Mckinley were not more than one hundred feet high. I must admit, it was fun, and I felt perfectly safe because my friend was thorough and professional in overseeing my ascent. I continued to climb.

When I reached about twenty feet up the rock. I realized that a one-hundred-foot-high rock is just a small mountain. I will admit that the view was great, but it was only great if I did not look straight down. At that point, my height fear began to kick in. My height fear is different than other fears I have experienced. I deduced that the "fight or flight" response does not apply to rock climbing. There was no one to fight, and there was nowhere to run, which left me with only the choice of continuing up the rock or going down in shame. I dislike shame more than heights.

At that point I also noticed that it was getting difficult to ascend because my legs were shaking just a little less than what could be termed violently. I hoped my friend did not notice the leg deal. To alleviate the leg shake, I was able to place myself in a position where I could lock my legs. This helped a lot, but it is difficult to climb rocks with locked legs.

Effectively avoiding the shame, I continued up the rock and made it all the way to the top. At the top, I noticed that my leg shaking stopped. I think it was because I found that rock climbing was pretty fun. In fact, I was comfortable enough climbing to make four more climbs that day; one was two hundred feet up. I was climbing like a person who had been climbing for an entire day.

Looking back, it was a pleasant experience because my friend was an expert rock climber. When all the rules are followed for an activity, it makes the activity enjoyable. I found this was true when using the Rope Saw techniques I learned while cutting branches. As I learned from my experiences, cutting branches did become somewhat enjoyable. It almost became like a game with me, but I had to follow the rules.

I made a hangman's knot using the carabiner and attached a Carabiner Safety Line to the carabiner in case I needed to undo the hangman's knot (see Figure 70a). With the Carabiner Safety Line attached to it, I pulled the hangman's knot tight around the Target Branch and routed the free end over the Security Branch. I pulled all the slack out of the Security Line and then tied it to a stationary object so that the Target Branch would not fall to the ground (see Figure 70b). It was a good idea to attach the Carabiner Safety Line because there were times when things went wrong, and I had to use the Carabiner Safety Line.

There are five steps when preparing to cut a Target Branch. Each step is a process. Ropes and lines need to be routed using increasingly larger spliced lines that may need to be encased in a tennis ball so that they will slide easily over a branch.

Routing the lines needed to be accomplished in a set order, or they would interfere with each other during a cut. It was important to pay close attention while setting everything up, or there was a risk that ropes would need to be removed and the process restarted. When everything was in place and ready for the cutting to begin (see Figure 72), I rechecked. Then, after the first two pulls of the saw, I checked everything again. The checking seemed unnecessary, but it was well worth the effort.

There were times when there was not a usable Security Branch above the Target Branch. In those cases, I selected an Offset Security Branch that could be used to direct the Target Branch away from the threatened structure after the Target Branch was cut. Any branch that would cause the Target Branch to swing away from threatened structures, and remain suspended, would work. The only difference in the steps to threading the Security Line, was that the security rope was threaded over a branch that was not directly above the Target Branch

Routing Security Line -
step 4 - Pull hangman's
knot tight around
Target Branch

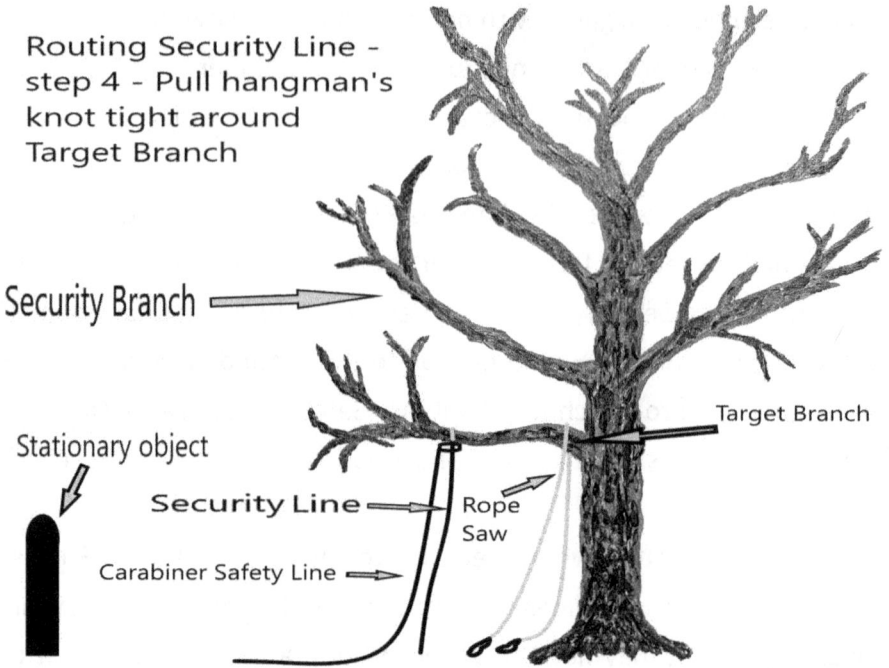

Security Branch ➡

Target Branch

Stationary object

Security Line ➡ Rope
Saw

Carabiner Safety Line ➡

Figure 70a

Routing Security Line -
step 5 - thread
Security Line over
Security Branch and
secure to stationary
object

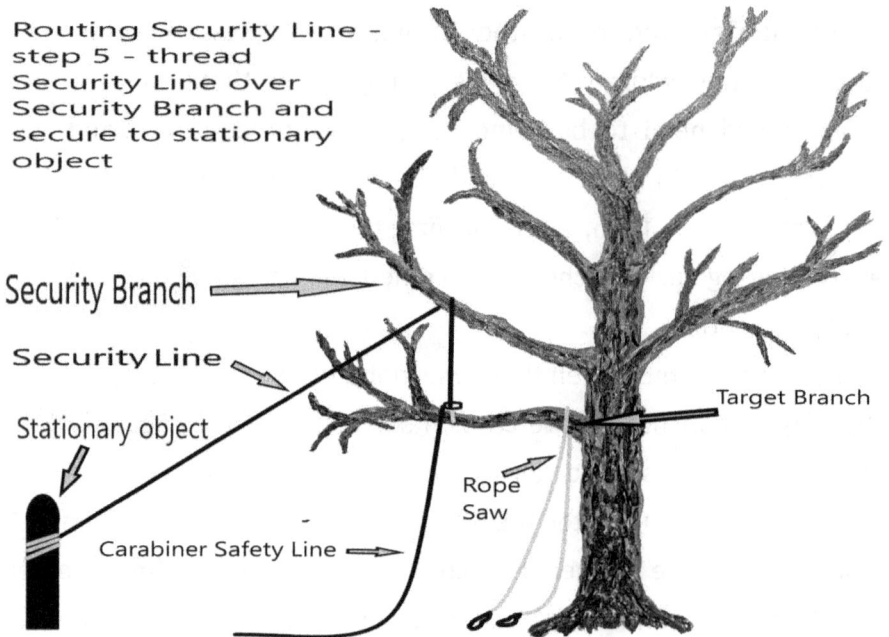

Security Branch ➡

Security Line ➡

Stationary object

Target Branch

Rope
Saw

Carabiner Safety Line ➡

Figure 70b

(see Figure 73).

I gave special attention to the length of the Security Line between the Security Branch and the Target Branch since the length controlled how far the Target Branch would be allowed to drop while it swung. Considering the length, the configuration needed to be studied closely to avoid any unforeseen issues with branches or structures. It was important that the security rope was strong enough to hold a Target Branch after it was cut and as it swung safely away from any threatened object (see Figure 74).

I cut branches that weighed over one hundred pounds. I needed to be sure the rope could manage the weight, so I bought the highest rated rope I could. What I ended up buying was a hundred feet of one-half inch rope. The rope is like that which cowboys use for roping calves. The rope I bought was not a lasso rope, but one that is used for general

Security Line Steps

1. Throw Security Line over the Target Branch
2. Attach a carabiner to the Security Line
3. Attach a carabiner Security Line to the carabiner
4. Pull hangman's knot tight around Target Branch
5. Throw Security Line over Security Branch
6. Secure Security Line to stationary object

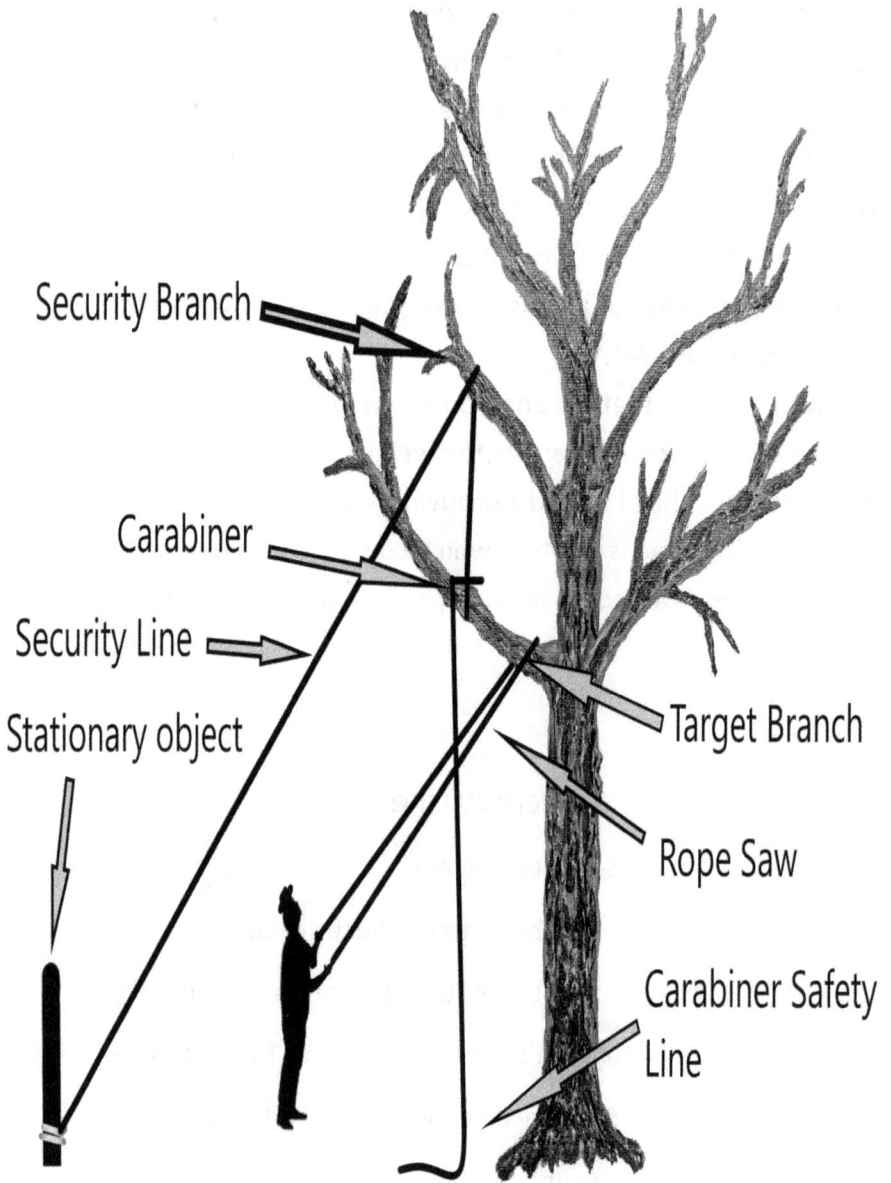

Security Branch

Carabiner

Security Line

Stationary object

Target Branch

Rope Saw

Carabiner Safety Line

Figure 72

purpose use and is made out of polyester. It was the nicest rope I had ever bought.

When I was young, I hit a cow with my car. It put my car out of commission for months. I have never been very knowledgeable about farm animals, and when the farmer referred to the cow as being a calf, I was surprised. The farmer said the calf weighed five-hundred pounds. I thought calves were the little fuzzy things that farmers carried in their

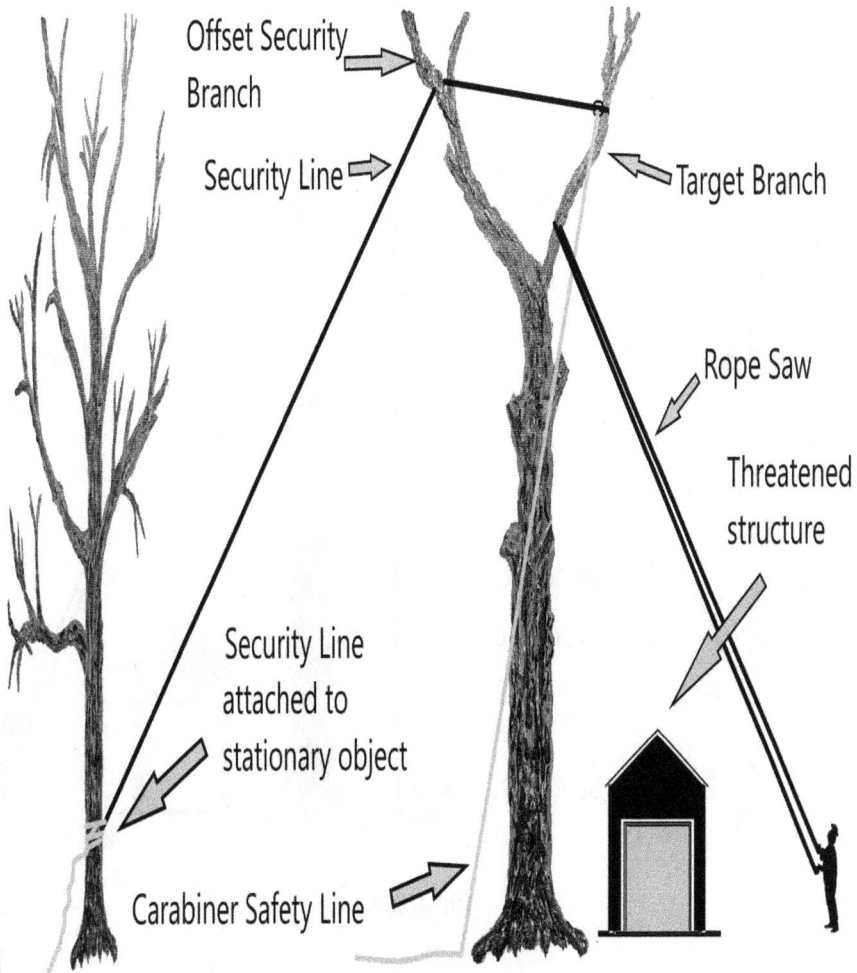

Offset Security Branch

Security Line

Target Branch

Rope Saw

Threatened structure

Security Line attached to stationary object

Carabiner Safety Line

Figure 73

arms to safety so they did not get hit by fire-breathing cars with hopped -up v-eights.

I never considered hitting the calf a useful experience until I bought the security rope. Because of my experience, I was sure the rope I bought would hold a hundred-pound branch, since cowboys used rope

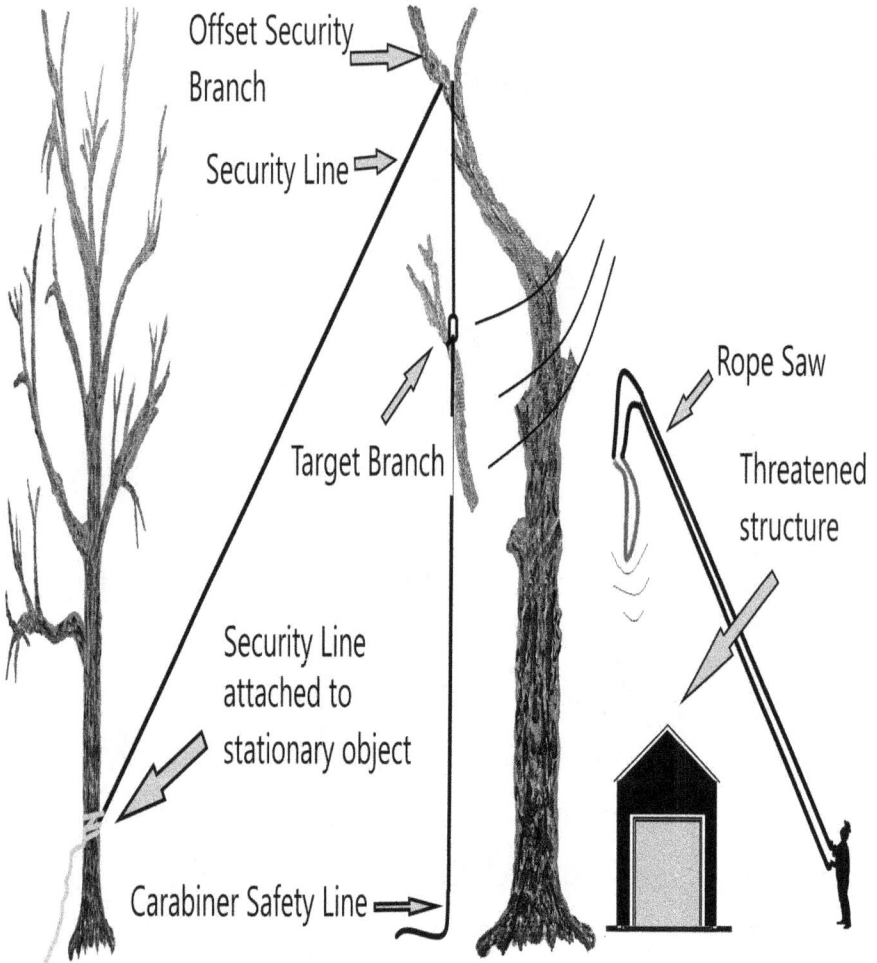

Offset Security Branch

Security Line

Rope Saw

Threatened structure

Target Branch

Security Line attached to stationary object

Carabiner Safety Line

Figure 74

just like it to hold five-hundred-pound calves.

Using my method of Rope Saw technology, tangles were a common occurrence. Stringing the ropes, however strange it sounds, required concentration. If I were not paying attention, it was easy to do something out of sequence or string a rope the wrong way and end up needing to unstring one or more ropes.

During one of the first experiences while working with a Bomb Branch. I found it necessary to somehow loosen and untie the security rope from the Target Branch. It seemed that it would not be difficult to do, but once the security rope was slip knotted to the Target Branch, it was almost impossible to untie without climbing the tree. And I do not climb trees.

I was fortunate that the Target Branch was low enough to reach and loosen the hangman's knot using the Stepladder Rake Maneuver. Another time when I needed to loosen a hangman's knot, I used an exceptionally long pole with a self-devised hook on it. The hangman's knot was high, but I was able to hook it and pull it loose and back to the ground.

It was obvious that there would be times I would need to undo a hangman's knot and restart the process. Loosening the hangman's knot with a rake or long pole was only possible because I was willing to invest hours trying to untie a knot in such a ridiculous manner. However, there were no other options, and the hangman's knot had to be removed to continue with the branch cutting process.

The Carabiner Safety Line was one of the best ideas I came up with (see Figure 76). Attaching a heavy safety line to the carabiner was easy

to do and worked very well. The only negative part of the safety line was that it added the extra line to the configuration. Because there were so many lines, it became customary practice to route lines in a proper sequence, then tie them out of the way until needed.

Getting back to my first Bomb Branch cut, I was almost confident that the complete configuration was workable and thinking that it likely would not result in any damage, I was completely ready to move forward with less than total confidence. Looking back, it seems there was something wrong with this logic.

With everything ready to go and the branch looming dangerously over the house, I took a long look at everything once again. I was fully aware that once I started cutting the branch, there was no turning back. By using the Security Line, the gamble was minimized, but it was still a gamble.

Throughout all my Rope Saw experience I always stopped to take time to ensure all the ropes were strung correctly. I found that the branches would do the craziest things when cut free from the tree. Luckily, none was fatal or damaging. Taking time to double check things

Carabiner Safety Line

Figure 76

was always well worth it. I would look up at the ropes, check how they were routed, then try to guess exactly what a branch would do when it was cut free. I often found an issue and needed to redo ropes before going forward.

There were times it would take an hour or more to cut one branch and I needed to rest. Sometimes it took hours to get the ropes in the right places. I once literally spent over nine hours to place one rope. There were times that I stopped and considered the madness of what I was doing and wondered if it was worth it.

With the Bomb Branch waiting patiently for me, I studied the configuration closely. I checked the position of all the ropes with my binoculars, and finding them soundly in place, I felt confident the cut would go well. I put the handholds on the Rope Saw Lines and prepared to start cutting.

I began pulling the Rope Saw Lines lightly – just enough so there was sawdust falling. I knew if I pulled the ropes too hard, they would cut too fast and would likely stick in the cut. I also knew that once I started cutting there was no turning back. I stopped once more to check the cut with my binoculars to ensure it was not a spiral cut and I found that it was not.

The branch looked to be about a foot in diameter. My heart was pounding because I knew this branch was heavy. I knew if it fell on the house, it would likely go through the roof. A sick feeling came over me as the saw cut further into the branch. There was no turning back and I knew there was nothing more I could do to make cutting the branch safer. I continued to cut.

After a good half hour of cutting, I became spent, so I took a timeout.

The saw was not dull, but the tree branch was dense and, although sawdust continuously fell as I was cutting, the saw was not moving through the branch very quickly.

Watching the clock, I realized I was nearing an hour of cutting time. I am guessing that, out of that hour, the actual cutting time was probably forty minutes. When my time spent cutting approached an hour and a half, the cut appeared to be almost completely through the branch. Again, I was amazed the branch had not broken off because of its weight, but it held tight. Looking at the cut with my binoculars I could see there was less than an inch left to cut through the branch. My heart was pounding, but I was not sure if it was because I was nervous about the branch breaking, or if it was because I was tired from pulling the Rope Saw for so long. I stopped to take one more break before the branch's grand finale.

Being rested and refreshed from my timeout, my heart continued to pound. No doubt, the whole thing was very nerve wracking. I began again to pull the Rope Saw with gentle pulls. I readied myself to bolt away from the branch. My main concern was that the Security Line would fail. If it did, it would be catastrophic. I tried not to think about it. Finally, after another fifteen minutes, which felt like an hour, I heard a slight crack.

While cutting branches, the branches would normally give a little warning and crack a little before they fell. Usually, there would be a small crack, then seconds later maybe another small crack, followed by a crack that could be heard around the neighborhood, then the branch would disengage from the tree and fall.

I prepared to run while ensuring my hands could slip easily from the handholds. Suddenly, there was an explosive crack, and the branch began to fall. I turned, shook off the handholds, and bolted away from the tree as small secondary branches shattered about me like shrapnel.

Secondary branches were always a concern. To protect the awning over the patio, I had placed sheets of plywood on top of it. I was glad I did because the secondary branches fell on the plywood.

Safely away from the drop zone, I turned to look and saw the Target Branch hanging safely from the Security Line. The cut was a complete success. The branch hung safely in the air held by the Security Line that I had anchored by coiling it around a nearby tree and tying a knot in it so that it could easily be undone. I undid the knot and fed line to the coil around the tree to let the branch drop slowly and safely to the ground (see Figure 81).

It was common practice for me to use a Security Line for almost all the branches I cut. The Security Line was necessary so I could slowly lower the branches to the ground rather than let them fall freely. Because the branches weighed so much, if one fell freely to the ground, it would be like a bomb going off; and not a small bomb.

When cutting a branch over a structure, and suspending it with a Security Line, the Carabiner Safety Line served not only as a safety backup to undo the hangman's knot, but I used it to guide the Target Branch away from any threatened structure while I slowly lowered the branch to the ground (see Figure 82).

With the Target Branch laying safely on the ground, I declared that my rope-saw-tennis-ball method was complete. During the following months, I used the method to safely remove many branches. The only downside of the method was that routing the lines took hours. Because of the line routing, it sometimes took days to remove one branch. I knew the time to remove branches was excessive, but the method was effective, safe, and when followed exactly, guaranteed that a falling branch would not damage the house, garage, or anything else.

As I continued cutting branches from the tree, I tried to think of a faster way to route the ropes. I knew there had to be a better way and I was confident that in time the idea would come to me. In the meantime, the Tennis Ball Method worked, and I was making progress.

Because I was making satisfactory progress, I did not want to break my pace by wasting time experimenting with any marginal ideas that would not work. I was waiting for the golden lightbulb to come on. I hoped it would not take long, and it did not.

To ensure each branch was cut safely and successfully, I recorded all the steps that I took while using the Tennis Ball Method for Free Fall Branch and Bomb Branches. I followed the steps carefully.

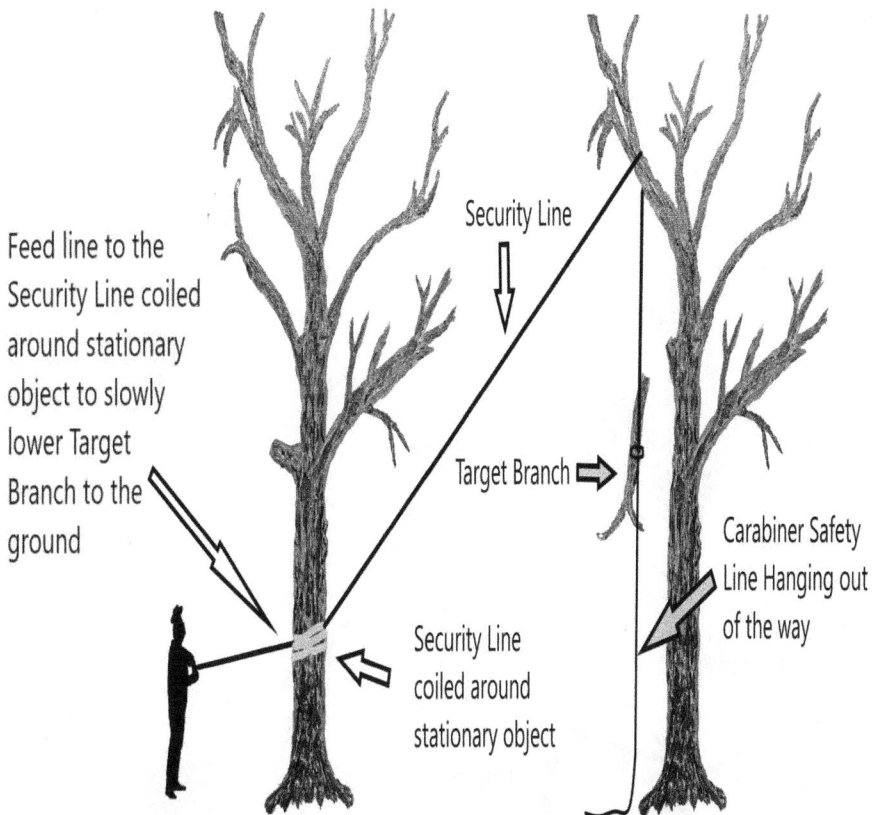

Feed line to the Security Line coiled around stationary object to slowly lower Target Branch to the ground

Security Line

Target Branch

Security Line coiled around stationary object

Carabiner Safety Line Hanging out of the way

Figure 81

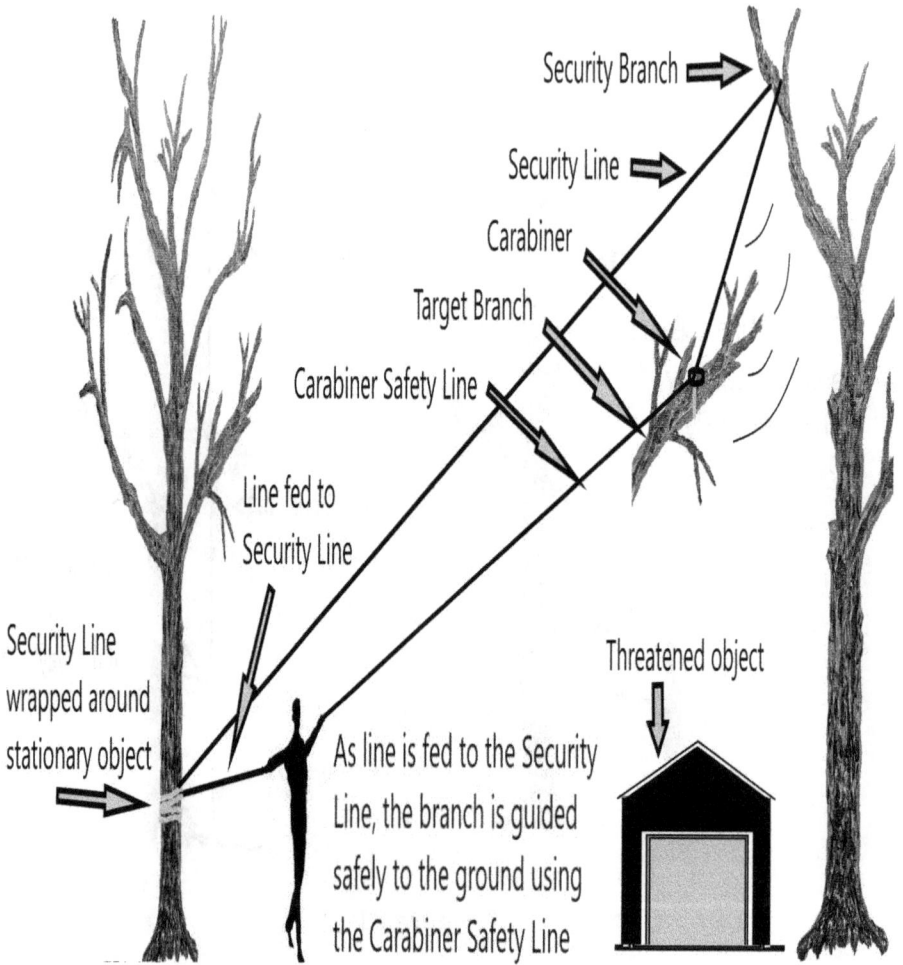

Security Branch ➡

Security Line ➡

Carabiner

Target Branch

Carabiner Safety Line ➡

Line fed to
Security Line

Security Line
wrapped around
stationary object ➡

Threatened object

As line is fed to the Security
Line, the branch is guided
safely to the ground using
the Carabiner Safety Line

Figure 82

Free Fall Branch Sequence Steps

1. Select the branch to cut
2. Using the Tennis Ball Method, route a fishing line over the Target Branch. Try to place the fishing line as close to the place on the branch where the cut will be made
3. If the fishing line is strong enough to pull the weight of the Rope Saw over the branch, disconnect the fishing line from the tennis ball and splice it to the Flip Tab line side of the Rope Saw. If the fishing line is not strong enough to pull the weight of the Rope Saw, use stronger braided nylon line in place of the fishing line
4. To ensure that the splice does not snag while pulling it over the branch, enclose it inside a tennis ball by making a slice half way around the tennis ball, and putting the splice inside the tennis ball as shown in Figures 36a, 36b and 36c
5. Pull the tennis ball containing the splice over the branch
6. With the Rope Saw Line over the branch near the place where the cut will be made, wag the line until the Rope Saw Line is exactly where the cut will be made. The Rope Saw itself should not be on the branch yet
7. Gently pull the Rope Saw into place, ensuring the teeth of the saw are facing down. Do not begin to cut the branch until everything is rechecked to ensure the saw is placed exactly where the cut will be made. Ensure that the cut will be made at the correct angle and that the cut will not result in a spiral cut (see Figure 41). Use binoculars to check the position and cut of the Rope Saw
8. Place the handholds on the Rope Saw Lines so that you can comfortably stand and pull the saw from side to side
9. Holding the handholds in a manner that allows you to release them instantly (see Figures 48a and 48b), begin to cut the branch by gently pulling the Rope Saw alternately left then right. You should see

sawdust falling from the cut. If not, the teeth of the saw may not be facing down. After two pulls, check the cut with binoculars. If the teeth are not facing down, pull the Rope Saw so it is just off the branch. Ensuring the Flip Tab side of the Rope Saw Line goes over the branch first, pull the Rope Saw back onto the branch so the Flip Tab flips the Rope Saw teeth down. It may take a few tries (see Figure 33b)

10. Begin pulling the saw again. After two pulls, stop and recheck the cut to ensure it is at the same angle on both sides of the branch and not a spiral cut (see Figure 41). If the Rope Saw is making a spiral cut, the saw should be removed and the cut restarted in a new position on the branch

11. Continue cutting, remaining ready to drop the handholds and move quickly away from the branch when it begins to drop to the ground

Bomb Branch Sequence Steps

1. Select the branch to cut

2. Using the Tennis Ball Method, cast a fishing line over the branch. Try to place the fishing line as close to the place on the branch where the cut will be made

3. If the fishing line is strong enough to pull the weight of the Rope Saw over the branch, disconnect the fishing line from the tennis ball and splice it to the Flip Tab line side of the Rope Saw. If the fishing line is not strong enough to pull the weight of the Rope Saw, use stronger braided nylon line in place of the fishing line

4. To ensure that the splice does not snag while pulling it over the branch, enclose it inside a tennis ball by making a slice one half way around the tennis ball, and enclosing the splice inside the tennis ball as shown in Figures 35a, 35b and 35c

5. Pull the tennis ball containing the splice over the branch

6. With the Rope Saw Line over the branch near the place where the cut will be made, wag the line until the Rope Saw Line is exactly where the cut will be made. The Rope Saw itself should not be on the branch yet

7. Gently pull the Rope Saw into place, ensuring the teeth of the saw are facing down. Do not begin to cut the branch until everything is rechecked to ensure the saw is placed exactly where the cut will be made. Ensure that the cut will be made at the correct angle and that the cut will not result in a spiral cut (see Figure 41). Use binoculars to check the position and cut of the Rope Saw

8. Place the handholds on the Rope Saw Lines so that you can comfortably stand and pull the saw from side to side. Place the Rope Saw Lines somewhere out of the way while the Security Line is threaded

9. Thread fishing line over the Target Branch using the Tennis Ball Method. Place the line away from the place where the Rope Saw is

placed

10. Splice fishing line to a Security Line that is strong enough to keep the branch from falling to the ground.

11. Thread the Security Line over the Target Branch using the fishing line. Enclose the splice inside a tennis ball if the line will likely snag on the branch when it is pulled over

12. Attach a carabiner to one end of the Security Line. Attach a braided nylon line (this is the Carabiner Safety Line) to the carabiner

13. Make a hangman's knot in the Security Line using the carabiner by threading one end of the Security Line through the carabiner

14. While feeding line to the Carabiner Safety Line, pull the hangman's knot in the Security Line tight around the Target Branch

15. Select a branch above the Target Branch that is strong enough to hold the Target Branch from falling to the ground. This is the Security Branch

16. With fishing line, use the Tennis Ball Method to thread the non-carabiner end of the Security Line over the Security Branch

17. Pull the Security Line as tight as possible so when the Target Branch breaks free from the tree, it remains suspended above any threatened structure. Wrap the end of the Security Line several times around a stationary object and tie securely

18. Place the Carabiner Safety Line out of the way. With everything now in place (See Figure 72), begin cutting

19. Holding the handholds in a manner that allows you to release them instantly (see Figures 48a and 48b), begin to cut the branch by gently pulling the Rope Saw alternately left then right. Sawdust should be seen falling from the cut. If not, the saw teeth may not be facing down. Check the teeth with binoculars. If they are not facing down, pull the Rope Saw so it is just barely off the branch. Ensure the Flip Tab line side of the Rope Saw is closest to the branch, then pull the Rope Saw onto the branch so the Flip Tab flips the Rope Saw teeth down. It may

take a few tries (see Figure 33b).

20. Begin pulling the saw again. After making two pulls, stop and recheck the cut to ensure it is at the same angle on both sides of the branch and not a spiral cut (see Figure 41).

21. If the Rope Saw is making a spiral cut, the saw should be removed and the cut restarted in a new position on the branch. If the saw cannot be pulled off the branch to be placed in another cut location, use the Saver Method described beginning on page 90

22. Continue cutting while being ready to drop the handholds and move quickly away from the branch as it falls from the tree. When the Target Branch is cut free from the tree, it should remain suspended in the air above any structure

23. Place yourself so that you can feed line to the Security Line looped around the stationary object. Begin to feed line to slowly lower the branch to the ground (see Figure 81). If necessary, use the Carabiner Safety Line to guide the branch away from any structures (see Figure 82)

There were times when a cut went so bad that I needed to remove the Rope Saw from the cut and start over. It was not an easy thing to do,

and it was sometimes impossible, which explains why there was an old rusting Rope Saw hanging in the tree for several years. Fortunately, Rope Saws are black, and they blend well with trees. Unfortunately, the part that hangs down does not blend, making a private backyard just that much nicer.

Throughout my tree trimming experiences, I only had to leave one Rope Saw hanging in the tree. When it happened, I had to devise a way to cut the Rope Saw Lines off the Rope Saw. They needed to be cut off where they were tied to the Rope Saw since their yellow color did not look well hanging in the tree. The Rope Saw hanging sadly by itself in the tree was bad enough. In addition to the embarrassment of the Rope Saw hanging in the tree, I had to endure months of replaying, in my mind, the frustrating experience of losing it; not to mention the memory of having to spend the money to buy a new Rope Saw. Because of the experience, I devised a method that I used to remove a Rope Saw when it became stuck or was making an improper cut - as in the case of a spiral cut. Here are the steps of the method. I call it the Saver Method.

Step One: When a Rope Saw became stuck, the first thing I did was to ensure there was a branch that was strong enough and higher than the branch where the Rope Saw was stuck. The Utility Branch had to be

positioned so that a rope could be placed on it directly over where the Rope Saw was stuck, since it needed to lift the Rope Saw out of the cut. If there was a branch I could use as a Utility Branch, I threw a one-fourth inch polyethylene rope (utility line) over the branch using the Tennis Ball Method (see Figure 90).

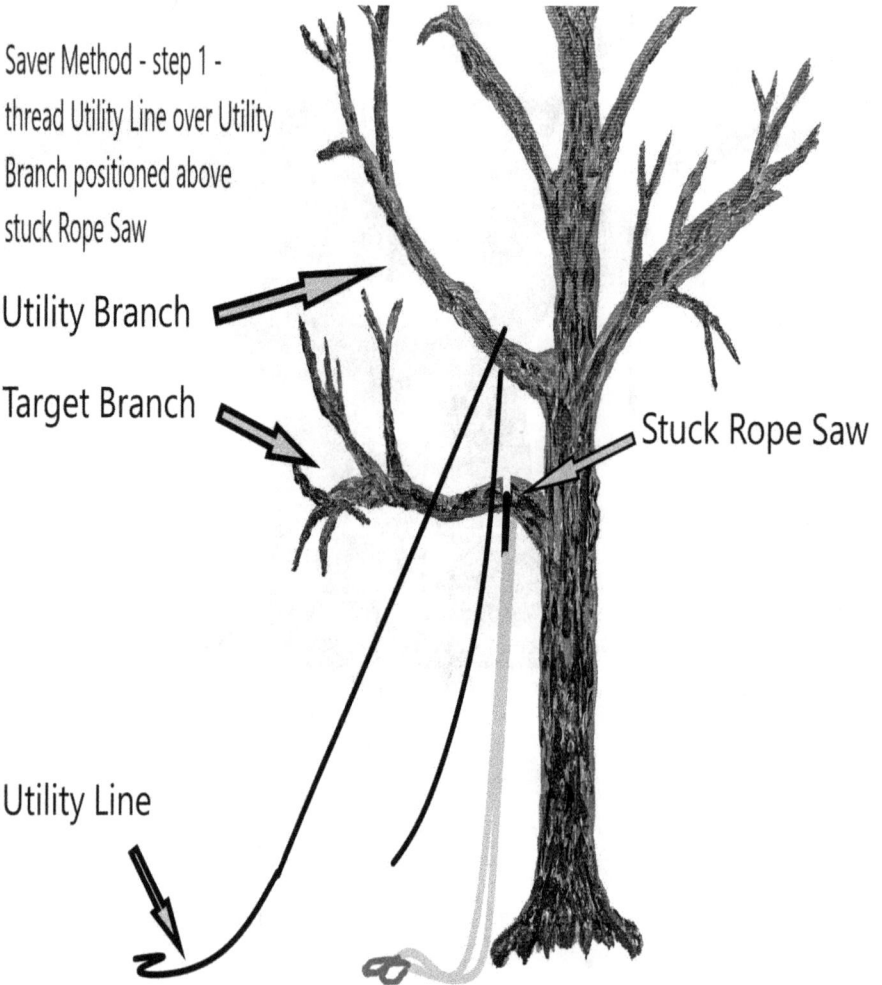

Saver Method - step 1 - thread Utility Line over Utility Branch positioned above stuck Rope Saw

Utility Branch

Target Branch

Stuck Rope Saw

Utility Line

Figure 90

Step Two: a carabiner was attached to the utility line (see Figure 91).

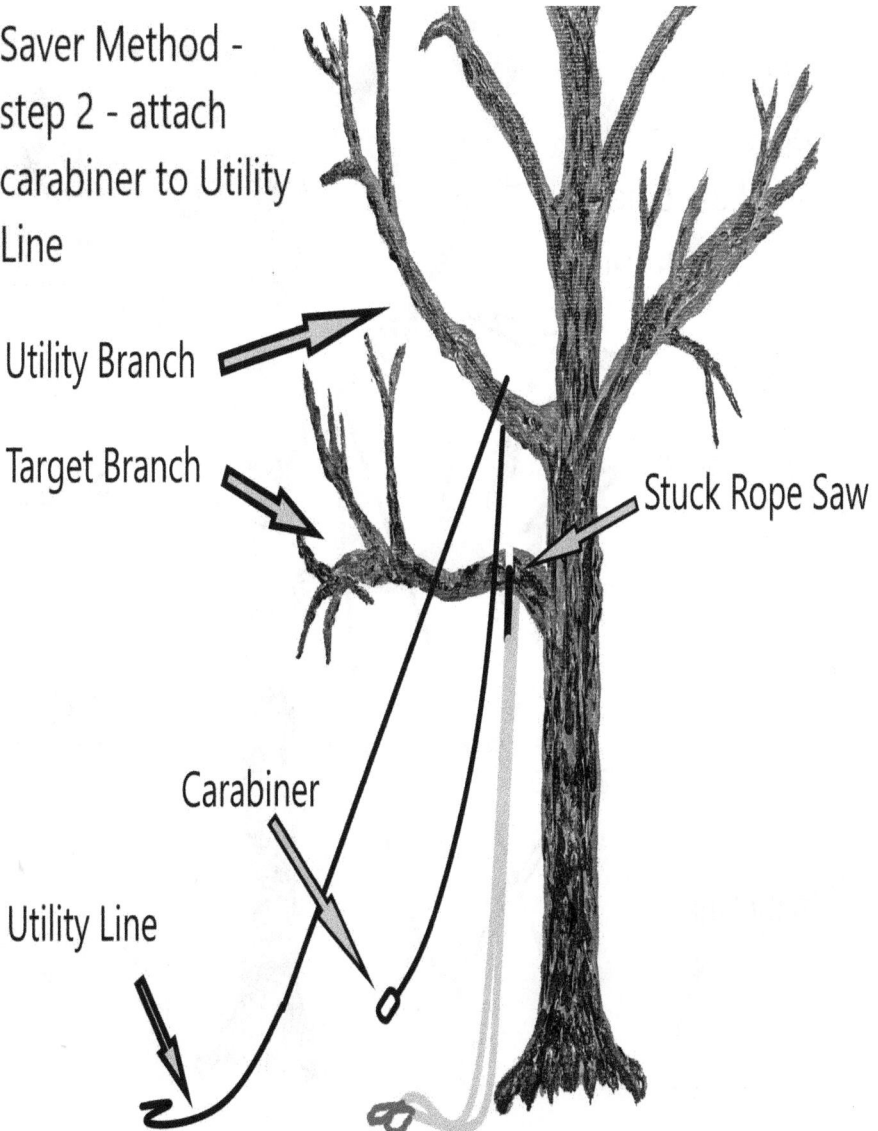

Figure 91

Step Three: The non Flip Tab line side of the Rope Saw was threaded through the carabiner on the utility line (see Figure 92).

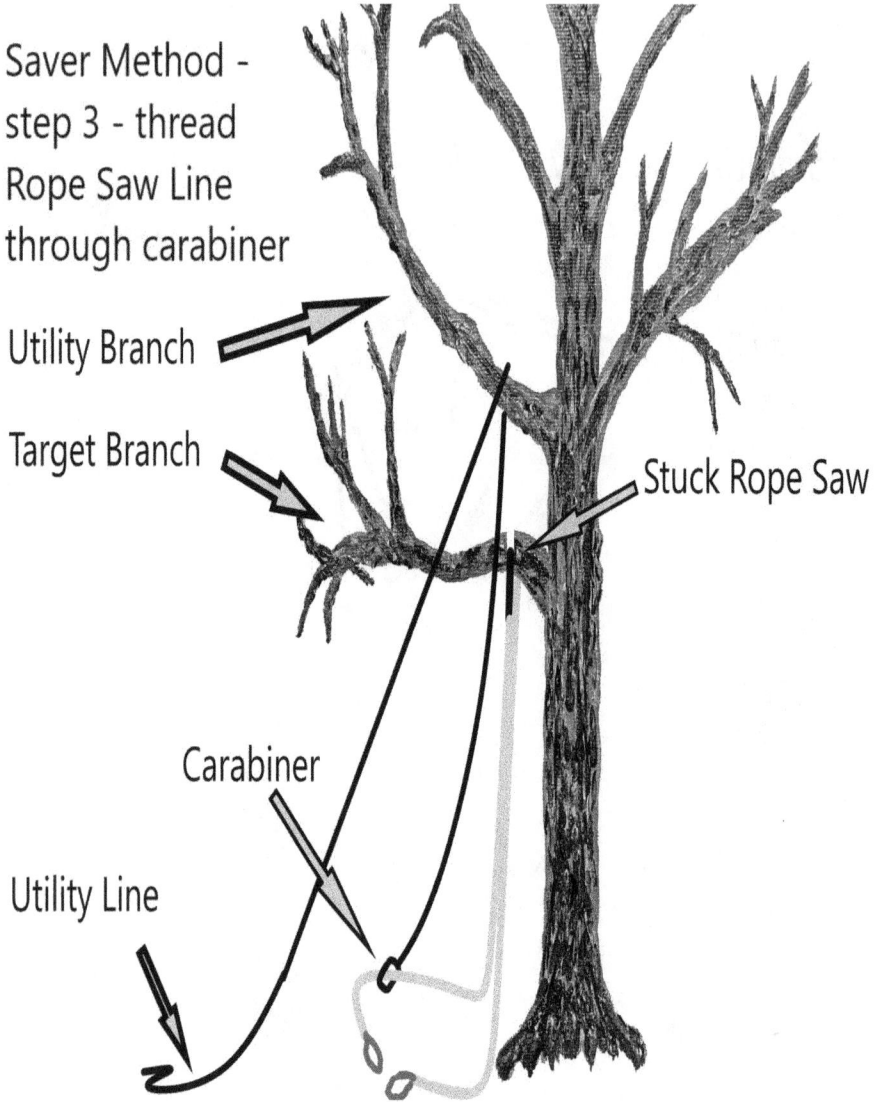

Figure 92

Step Four: A Carabiner Safety Line was attached to the carabiner. (see Figure 93).

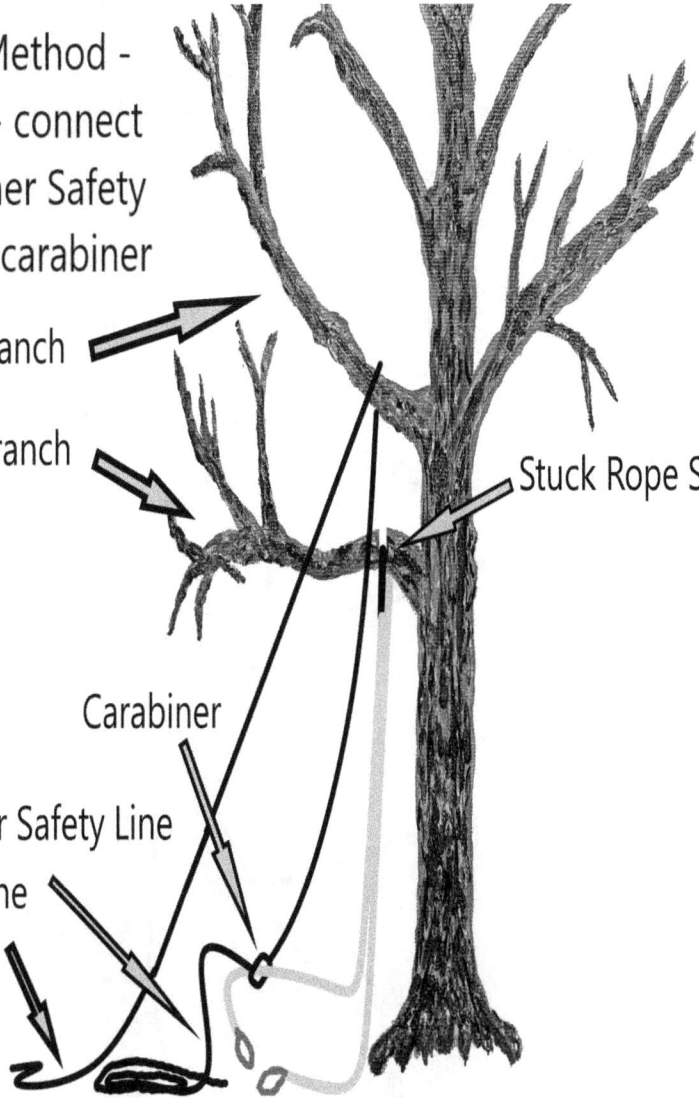

Saver Method - step 4 - connect Carabiner Safety Line to carabiner

Utility Branch

Target Branch

Stuck Rope Saw

Carabiner

Carabiner Safety Line

Utility Line

Figure 93

Step Five: While holding the Rope Saw Line, that was threaded through the carabiner, the utility rope was pulled so that the carabiner traveled up the Rope Saw Line and so the Rope Saw was pulled into the carabiner. The utility line was then used to lift the Rope Saw out of the cut (Figure 94).

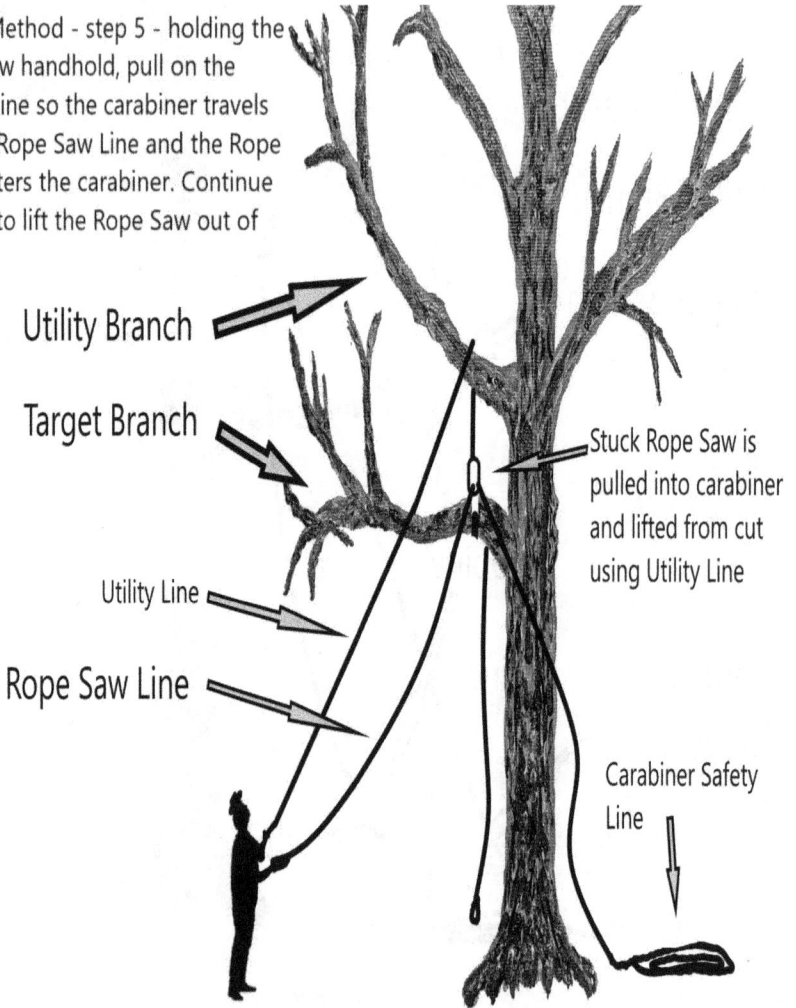

Saver Method - step 5 - holding the rope saw handhold, pull on the Utility Line so the carabiner travels up the Rope Saw Line and the Rope Saw enters the carabiner. Continue to pull to lift the Rope Saw out of the cut

Utility Branch

Target Branch

Stuck Rope Saw is pulled into carabiner and lifted from cut using Utility Line

Utility Line

Rope Saw Line

Carabiner Safety Line

Figure 94

To remove the Rope Saw from the cut sometimes required jiggling and yanking. When a Rope Saw becomes stuck, it was usually because it was wedged in the cut in an unusual angle. If the Saver Method did not work using the non-Flip Tab line side of the Rope Saw, I tried it on the Flip Tab side. Using the Flip Tab side was a last resort, since allowing the Flip Tab to enter the carabiner sometimes made the utility line unretrievable. The Carabiner Safety Line made removing the saw from the carabiner possible, however, when using the Flip Tab side, the Flip Tab would likely not pass back through the carabiner.

6
The Golden Lightbulb

Cutting up the branches into fireplace-size logs was the best way I found to dispose of the branches. I would stack the logs up in an out of the way place in the backyard in case we needed to heat the house with the wood during a power outage. It did not make any difference that losing power was unlikely. We live in the middle of town near gas stations, grocery stores, banks and coffee shops. I knew it was not a big deal to the gas stations, grocery stores or banks if the power went out, but there was no way the public would put up with the power going out at the coffee shop.

The wood pile was growing nicely and would have impressed even a weather hardened backwoodsman from Alaska. One issue that I am sure Alaskan backwoodsmen are not concerned about is mice. I found that woodpiles are the preferred homesites of mice. Other than heights, I dislike spiders and mice with a passion. If I see a spider in the house, it wrecks my day; if I see a mouse, it wrecks my week. Getting rid of spiders is easy, getting rid of mice is a whole different story.

We have not had a mouse in the house, or garage, for a long time. Once, we saw a mouse scurry across a room in the house – in the daytime. This was enough to sell the house at an extremely low price. Fortunately, I dislike moving even more than spiders and mice.

Through the years I have become a good mouse catcher. So, I began to set traps in the house. I was confident that the mouse got in through the foundation, so my prime mouse target area was the basement. We have a crawl space, and the mice like that area best, so I strategically placed my first trap in the crawl space.

I always use peanut butter for mousetrap bait for two reasons; mice love peanut butter better than life; and I do too. So, after enjoying crackers slathered with peanut butter, and kicking them up a notch by sprinkling them with chocolate chips, I baited up the trap and set it in the crawlspace. The mice did not get any chocolate chips. I decided another mousetrap in the crawlspace would be good, so I headed to the garage to get one.

To my horror, and I do not use the word lightly, when I returned to the crawl space, I had already caught a mouse. I thought, okay, I am really a good mouse trapper, and I caught that sole house invading mouse in a record time. So, I calmed down, reset the trap, and added the other trap.

Done with the crawl space, I put two traps upstairs in strategic locations. When I finished, I could not help myself, I had to check the traps in the crawl space again. I do not know why I had to subject myself to the torture, I am a firm believer in the happiness found through ignorance, but I just had to look. When I did, horror just did not work for me anymore, it was fright; I had caught another mouse.

Shaking nervously, which reminded me of rock climbing, I reset the traps and went outside for fresh air. I knew there were not any mice outside. After another ten minutes, I did it again; I checked the traps and found two more mice. It was all I could do to not scream like a girl. The only good thing about the whole ordeal was that I only caught four, then there were no more for days. At that point, I took a vacation from tree trimming to deal with the mouse problem. I admit, I would rather trim trees with a Rope Saw than deal with mice.

I rigged up my nine-iron golf club with a mirror so I could do a micro inspection of my house's foundation. Using every hole plugging material I could find at the hardware store; I hermitically sealed my house. I was careful to ensure enough oxygen could get into the house to support life – but only the minimum needed.

If there was any benefit to the whole mouse experience, it was that I realized that woodpiles in the backyard are not good. The mice will quickly outgrow the wood pile and will move into the house if there is any conceivable way for them to get in. There is no longer a wood pile in my backyard. If the power goes out, I will go to the coffee shop.

The tree was big enough to keep me occupied with cutting dead branches for years to come. It was fortunate that the branches that died were always around one foot in diameter, with fourteen inches being the largest.

All the branches were very heavy, exceptionally long, and always had many small branches. Their size and weight always commanded my respect. I only cut larger branches when it was necessary, and I made sure to remove all the small branches from them prior to cutting them. Cutting large branches would take days because caution was always the rule when using the Rope Saw.

The one glaring issue that remained with my Tennis Ball Method, was the time it took to route lines. I remember only once when I hit a branch exactly where I wanted it to go on the first try. It amazed me that it always took so long to get the rope in the exact place I wanted it. Looking back, it took so long because I was trying to throw a tennis ball over thirty feet up into a tree filled with branches and leaves, with a tangle of string tied to it, while trying to hit a six-inch target.

The number of throws grew because of the number of times I was standing on the fishing line attached to the tennis ball. The braided fishing line is hard to see laying on the ground. I had to pull and lay enough length of line on the ground so the tennis ball could reach the target. The pile of string on the ground was a snag waiting to happen. Being careful not to stand on the line was a constant concern.

I cannot really say how long it was before the new idea popped into my head. What led me into the idea was that I thought of how a golf ball would be easier to throw because it has more mass. A golf ball's size and weight make it ideal for traveling distances.

I am an occasional golfer. I have a bad slice. But I know I have a slice, so I always aim thirty yards to the left of wherever I want the ball to go. It works for me. When I par a hole, the hardest part is not looking surprised, which is not a problem for whoever I am golfing with.

I have a good supply of golf balls in my golf bag. I have only once, that I can remember, played a whole round of golf using the same golf ball. Usually, by the time I have golfed nine holes, I am using old range golf balls that I found. Some of the golf balls I use are waterlogged, but it does not hurt my score one bit. I grabbed a couple golf balls and tried throwing them at a branch. They were easier to throw, but I could not throw them any more accurately than the tennis balls, and I had no clue how to attach a fishing line to one.

My first idea was to cut a string sized channel all the way around the golf ball and then tie the fishing line around the ball in the channel. It sounded good, but I had never tried cutting a small channel all the way around a golf ball. I was surprised to find that it is not particularly easy. After a couple tries with a hobby knife, I found out that it was actually dangerous, which fit right in to all my other Rope Saw activities.

A channel would not make it easy to disconnect and reconnect the fishing line to the golf ball, which was something I had to do often to avoid tangles or undo a tangle. I knew there was an idea just waiting to pop, so I went to my garage workbench to look through the multitude of hardware items I had gained through the years. After searching, I found the perfect piece of hardware, an eyehook.

It was much easier to screw an eyehook (see Figure 101a) into a golf ball then to cut a channel around it; and it was safer too. Tying the fishing line to the eyehook was simple (see Figure 101b) and it would be easy to undo the string and retie it so I could fix and undo tangles.

Armed with my new golf ball configuration, I set the tennis ball aside and began throwing the golf ball with the fishing line attached. It was completely different throwing the golf ball. It was easy to overthrow because the weight was more compacted, and the ball was smaller. It would go farther and faster than the tennis ball did, which meant it was easier to overthrow, and so it would go farther up into the tree.

Consequently, the fishing string got tangled more. However, the added distance was worth the risk of getting the line tangled, and the tangles were easy enough to deal with if the string did wind around any branches.

If the line did not get wound around a branch, I could either cut the line, and just pull the line through the branches, or I could very carefully and gently pull the ball back through the snags. If the ball were not pulled carefully it would begin to swing, and then wind the fishing line around a branch (see Figures 102 and 103). Once the line was wound around a branch, if the branch was large and too strong to be pulled down with the ball, the only thing to do was pull hard enough to break the fishing line. After the fishing line broke, if lucky, the ball fell from the tree and the string could be pulled down. If unlucky, the golf ball would remain tangled in the tree and another golf ball had to be rigged with fishing line.

Some stranded golf balls were not easy to see up in the tree; others were extremely easy to see and would hang boldly and contemptuously in the tree for anyone in my backyard to see. I am not sure how, but the tangled balls eventually became untangled and fell from the tree. It would take weeks - if it happened at all. It was humorous to find a disentangled golf ball lying in the yard. It was like sweet revenge and regaining a golf ball was like winning the Rope Saw lottery.

Using the golf ball was a definite improvement over using the tennis ball. Disconnecting and reconnecting the golf ball was much easier than disconnecting and reattaching the tennis ball. It was a simple matter of cutting the string from the eyehook on the golf ball and retying it. Unlike the tennis ball, the line would occasionally and unexpectedly slip through the ball since the knot was all that kept it from doing so; the fishing line stayed attached to the golf ball eyehook. I tried tying the fishing line around the tennis ball so the knot would not pull out, but it

Figure 101a   Figure 101b

took more time than using the needle-nose pliers, and was much more difficult to disconnect if the tennis ball was tangled in the tree.

One of my main tools for working with tennis balls and golf balls was the needle-nose pliers. I used the needle-nose to pull the string through the tennis ball as shown in Figure 32a and 32b. Pushing the point of the needle-nose completely through the tennis ball, I grabbed the fishing

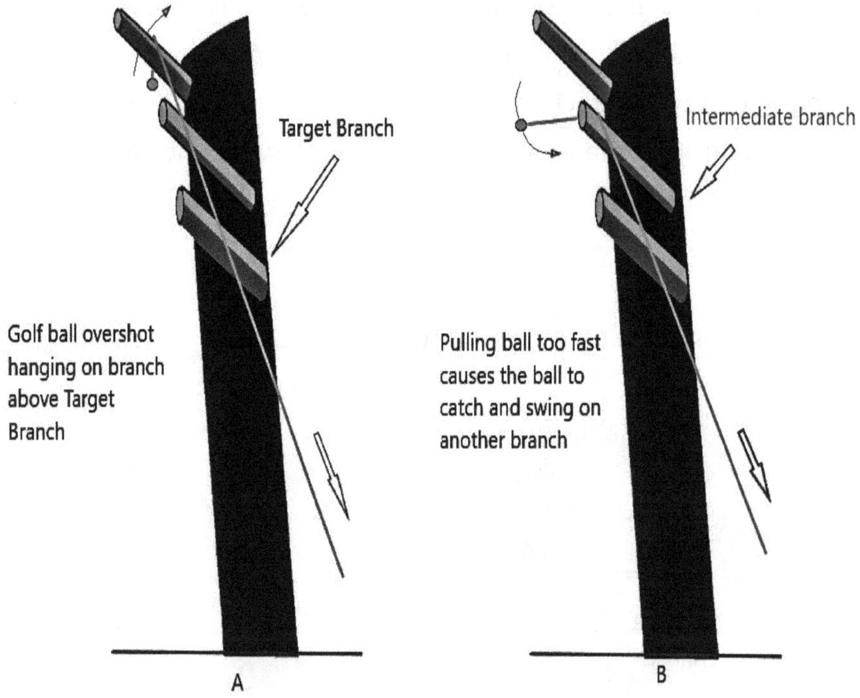

Target Branch

Intermediate branch

Golf ball overshot hanging on branch above Target Branch

Pulling ball too fast causes the ball to catch and swing on another branch

A

B

Figure 102

line with the needle-nose and pulled it all the way through the tennis ball. Then I tied a large enough knot in the fishing line to keep it from being pulled back through the tennis ball. When using the tennis ball, or the golf ball, I used the wire cutting capability of the needle-nose to cut the line from the tennis ball or the eyehook. The needle-nose was an all-

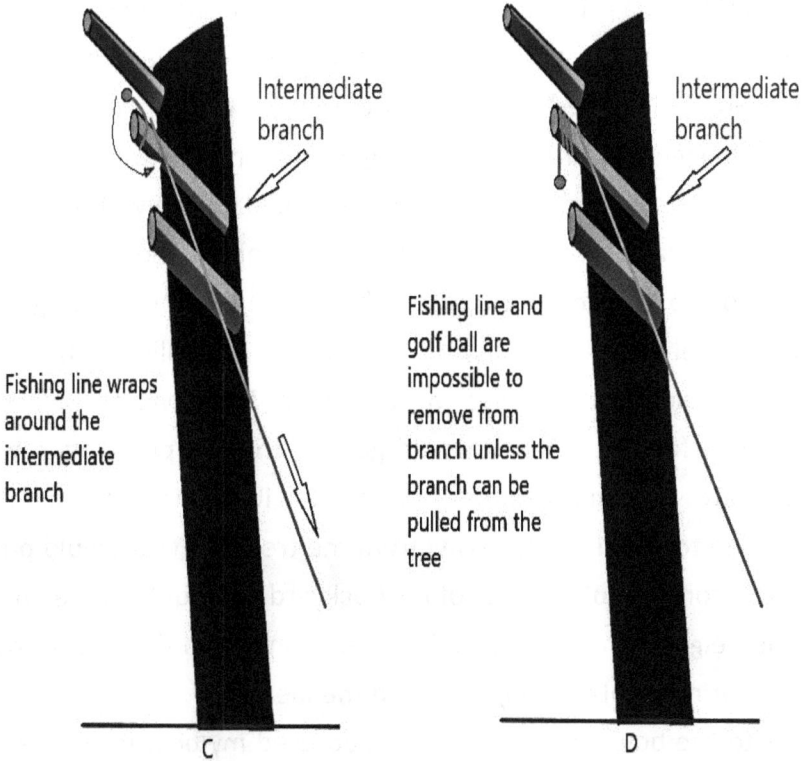

Intermediate branch

Fishing line wraps around the intermediate branch

Intermediate branch

Fishing line and golf ball are impossible to remove from branch unless the branch can be pulled from the tree

C

D

Figure 103

around useful tool for cutting branches with the Rope Saw.

Controlling the golf ball was easier than controlling the tennis ball. As much as I liked using the golf ball, it was still taking an extraordinarily long time to hit the exact spot where I wanted to cut branches. I was getting tired of how long it was taking to get a line routed, and after deep thought it occurred to me that it was all because of how inaccurately I was throwing the balls. This seems obvious, but it narrowed the issue to accuracy. The challenge was how to improve the precision of my throws.

It was time again to think through the issue at hand and produce a solution. My first idea was a wild one. I thought of a friend who made a potato gun and showed me how it worked. He would ram a potato in the gun barrel and charge the firing chamber with a good shot of hairspray; aim high and fire it. The potato would launch with a bang and go fast and straight into the sky where he aimed. I thought, if I could make a potato gun and put a rifle sight on it, I could ram the golf ball into the barrel and launch it with the accuracy of a military sniper rifle. The only problem with the idea was the range. There was no way I could control how far the golf ball would go. My friend's potato gun would shoot potatoes about one hundred yards.   It occurred to me that I just needed to stand farther away from the tree, but that would put me out of the comfortable privacy of my backyard. It would also be an issue with the neighbors or the police if I were standing in the street or their backyard firing a potato gun, so I nixed the idea.

Back to the bow and arrow idea. I had used my bow for bow fishing often. I also shot target archery and was able to put arrows into a ten-inch bullseye consistently. Bow fishing arrows are heavier than regular arrows so they do not travel as far as regular arrows. A bow fishing arrow, with a string tied to it, travels slower than a regular arrow. I rationalized that the experience I had with my brother-in-law's bow was because of error on my part. So, if I could attach the fishing line to a bow fishing arrow; which was a perfectly normal thing to do, and then control the distance the arrow traveled by limiting how far I drew the bow string back, then I had the solution I was looking for. It was worth a try. Besides, my backyard was private, and I would be shooting straight up. What could go wrong?

I got my bow out and rigged it up with a fishing arrow. I connected the string, stripped enough string from the spool to ensure the arrow could travel up to the branch I was going to aim at, notched the arrow and pulled the bow string back ever so slightly. Then came the answer to my question; there was no way to pull the bow string back slightly enough to only have the arrow go a short distance. The arrow took off like a rocket and traveled through the tree branches without being deflected at all. The arrow went flying above the tree and headed toward the neighbor's backyard.

While the arrow was still in the air, I relived the experience I had with my brother-in-law's bow and mechanical release. Everything began to move in slow motion. I thought of everything that could go wrong; would the arrow stick into the roof of their garage, their deck, their car?

Regret grew as the arrow flew higher into the air. I vowed that I would never try anymore wild ideas. Then miraculously the arrow jolted to a stop as it ran out of string. Providence had saved me again! The arrow fell harmlessly to the ground, on my side of the fence.

Relieved, I took a break and sat quietly for awhile. I replayed the near miss in my head a few times and conceded that it was a crazy thing to do. I amended my vow to stop doing crazy things after I finished trimming the tree.

Looking back, the potato gun was a wild idea. The bow fishing arrow was not as wild, but it was right up there. I was struggling with the problem. I knew there was an answer, but I did not have a clue what it was.

I considered that I would have to be satisfied with what I had. The underhand method of swinging the ball, like what David did with his sling to bean Goliath, might just be the best I could do. I wondered how David launched the stones so accurately. Of course, David was herding sheep in the middle of nowhere. He did not have a cell phone to play games on, or a transistor radio to listen to the current top forty. He had all the time in the world to practice. He was the best slingshot shot in the world at the time he beaned Goliath. Then it occurred to me. David used a slingshot! In this day and age, no one uses a slingshot like David did. We have modern slingshots that are state-of-the-art slingshots that can be aimed! I packed up all my Rope Saw paraphernalia and headed to the sporting goods store.

I had not had a slingshot since my pre-teen years. Dennis the Menace always had one hanging out of his back pocket, and I liked Dennis; not just because he was fun to watch, but because we thought alike. Carrying a slingshot was the closest thing to packing heat a kid could do back then. Consequently, carrying a slingshot was also the fastest way to get into trouble.

My folks knew how the gears turned in my head. The slingshot was maybe not a good idea, so they got me a BB gun. Slingshots are more powerful than BB guns. I am not sure why, maybe because rocks are bigger than BB's.

After visiting three sporting goods stores, and finding no slingshots, I was beginning to think I had wrecked it for everyone when I was a kid. I was finally able to find a slingshot at a farm supply store. It made perfect sense; farm kids always had all the fun.

The choice was not great, they had only one generic slingshot. But it was one nice slingshot. It was built well and instead of measly rubber bands, it had strong rubber tubes that stretched nicely and would obviously shoot a projectile with an elevated level of kinetic energy. It was a little scary that what had been a toy for me as a boy, had developed into a dangerous weapon.

A store employee noticed me looking at the slingshot. He pointed out that you could not buy a slingshot in city limits because it was illegal for stores to sell them. The farm store was not in city limits.

It was news to me that you could not buy a slingshot in city limits. Eventually, it will be illegal to transport a slingshot across a city border. They will set up slingshot inspection stations where everyone crossing the city border will be searched before being allowed to enter. Luckily, there are no inspection stations yet, so I bought one.

When I got back to the backyard, I resisted the urge to grab a rock to see if I was still a talented slingshot artist. But I figured there was no reason to cause any unnecessary problems since I had enough necessary ones.

I gave the new slingshot a test stretch. I could not help but think that, if I had a slingshot like this when I was a kid, I would be in jail now. The slingshot pulled smoothly and released cleanly. The hand grip felt comfortable and it felt like a precision instrument that was as precise as any fine target rifle. I loaded up a golf ball and gave the slingshot a short pull back and let the golf ball fly. The golf ball flew safely out to about twenty feet.

The slingshot's leather sling was too small for the golf ball to fit in it. Normally a rock or marble would be wrapped in the sling, then, while holding the rock or marble in the leather sling with the thumb and forefinger, the sling would be pulled back and released to shoot the projectile. Since the golf ball was too big to be wrapped in the leather sling, I had to grasp the golf ball between my thumb and forefinger to pull it back and shoot it (see Figure 109).

Grasping the golf ball instead of the leather sling degraded the accuracy of the shot. For the best accuracy the projectile (in this case the golf ball) needed to be exactly centered in the sling so that the total force was applied directly and evenly to the golf ball. When grasping the golf ball to pull the slingshot back, I found it difficult to hold the ball so that the force of the slingshot was directed to the exact center of the golf ball. The problem also affected distance because the total force of the slingshot was not being completely applied to the golf ball.

Because the golf ball was too big to be grasped and centered in the leather sling, the accuracy and distance was not as good as it could have been. But it was still much more precise than swinging the tennis ball in a circle and releasing it.

Another concern was the fishing string. I had to be careful while laying the string in the slingshot so that it would not hang up on the slingshot arms when I shot it. It was not serious when it did snag on the slingshot, but it always spoiled the shot. Allowing the free feed of the fishing line was always important, since if the line did not feed it would wreck the shot attempt.

Every shot attempt took several minutes to set up correctly, so it was important to make each shot count. Shooting was also strenuous and became tiresome after making numerous missed shots. It was important to keep missed shots at a minimum.

When tired, I was more apt to snag the line or miss a shot. It is always the best practice to take your time while shooting a line. I found the more relaxed I was, the better the chance I had of hitting the mark. Shooting the golf ball was better, but it needed good concentration so that the ball was held and released in the slingshot exactly right. I knew the golf ball was a good idea, but it was just not good enough. I had to find a better way.

There was one added concern with the slingshot. The slingshot instructions said the rubbers on the slingshot needed to be checked occasionally to ensure they were not in danger of breaking, since, if they did break, they might injure the user.

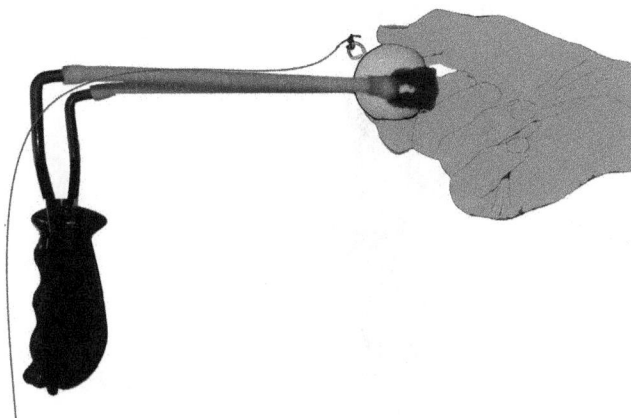

Figure 109

7
The Wall

I was making better headway with the golf ball eyehook method. I was hitting the correct place on the branches more often, but shooting the golf ball in the slingshot, because of the way I had to hold it, just felt wrong. In addition to wrong, it took too much concentration to make even a marginal shot. If I held the golf ball just a little wrong, it would mess the shot up. The leather was just not large enough to hold the golf ball correctly and it was causing me to waste shots.

Trimming the tree had turned into a major undertaking for me. The time I put into taking care of the tree was significant. Moby Tree was losing the war, but the battles were time consuming. I was beginning to understand what Captain Ahab felt like. Although I was not fixated on the tree, it was a task that had to be done. I had too much time invested to call it quits, and there were still dead branches that needed cutting.

Surprisingly, trimming Moby Tree was not the wildest project I have ever taken on. The wildest was by far the wall.

111

The wall refers to the shorter of two retaining walls in front of my house. The wall is about thirty feet long. It is beautifully made of natural hand carved stones. The folks who had the wall built in the nineteen forties spared no expense in building the retaining walls on the property. They are beautiful and in exceptionally good condition, except for one which was leaning a little.

I have spent quite a bit of time studying walls since buying the house. I would like to say it is because I am genuinely interested in learning about walls, but it has much more to do with frugality. Frugality is the nice term we all use for cheap. What it actually means is; working unbelievably hard and long hours while struggling to mimic the appearance and expertise of a professional who would do the same job in a fraction of the time and at a fraction of the cost.

It is not really that I am cheap, it is simply hard for me to stand around doing nothing while someone else is working. I know it sounds strange, but I do not mind working hard. It does not make any sense to me to go to the gym and work out while I can get a better workout doing wild stuff at home. However, looking back, whenever I have done something wild, I have always made a firm pledge that I would never do it again. I think it takes extra time for slow learners to join health clubs. The wall project was one of those wild ideas. In defense of myself, it was not completely my idea to do it.

As I said, the wall leaned a little bit. I am not sure how much it leaned. I did not measure how far it was off a ninety-degree angle with the world. All I know is when I looked at it, I could tell it was not straight. The other walls were straight. That is probably why the one wall leaning bothered me.

It did not always bother me. Just whenever I looked at it. It was easy to rationalize that it was not leaning very much. But really, when a wall is leaning enough to notice that it is leaning, it is leaning more than it should. Driving by the front of the house, it was not easy to tell the wall was leaning. Walking down the sidewalk it was easy to tell. No one mentioned any problems with the wall, so I thought it was a personal hangup.

I put time into thinking about how to fix the wall. One idea involved burying railroad ties in the yard and then running long bolts through the wall into the ties. Then by tightening the bolts, it would pull the wall back straight. It was a theory. I am not that fond of theories; especially ones that are not proven, which are all of them. I checked on where I could buy railroad ties and found a couple options. I did not plan to start

fixing the wall, but I knew that someday I would get to a point where I could no longer restrain myself, so I set out to learn more about leaning walls.

Masonry has always appealed to me, except for the part about how much work it is to get rocks. I have had visions of a semi-truck backed up in my driveway unloading large boulders. After the boulders were unloaded, I would carve the rocks into brick sizes. The fun part would be when I assembled whatever I was going to build. I have always had a tough time getting past the part about carving the boulders.

The second idea I came up with was right up my alley. It would be a lot of work, it had numerous unknowns, it was something I was not willing to share with any of my friends for fear of ridicule, and it seemed like an impossible feat to accomplish. In other words, it was perfect.

The plan was to disassemble the wall one rock at a time, then reassemble it so that it was not leaning. I would take a picture of the wall and number each rock on the picture. Then, after I removed a rock from the wall, I would write the corresponding number on the back of the rock with a magic marker. After all the rocks were removed, I would use the picture, with the numbers on the rocks, to reassemble the wall without the lean.

There were challenges; I did not know how I would disassemble the wall and, when I got a rock free from the wall, I was not sure it was possible to remove the cement from the rock. I was hoping that I just had to hit it with a hammer, and it would fall off. I had no experience with cement, and I just did not know how well it stuck to rocks.

Another challenge was that I had never built a wall. I did not know what cement I would use to hold the rocks together. I did not know if I had the ability to rebuild the wall without a lean. I had ideas about running plumb lines but, honestly, I had never worked with plumb lines. There were other challenges, but the challenges were not concerning since I had not committed to doing the job.

I bought a masonry book and it was excellent. It confirmed that my idea to rebuild the wall would be a real backbreaker. Unfortunately, it still looked kind of fun, and in my unrealistic estimation, it was doable. At least I thought it was doable. The book explained what tools and materials I would need to tear down and rebuild the wall. I did not have any of the tools, so I was delighted that I would get to make a trip to the hardware store to do a little shopping.

Then the day came. Someone, other than me, pointed out that the wall was leaning and that it needed to be fixed. I was hoping that day would never come and that the lean was all in my head, but the lean was now confirmed by someone else, and I no longer had any choice but to fix the wall.

It occurred to me that there might be men that fixed walls for a living so they could feed their families. I felt morally obliged to do my part to help them, so I began looking for a company that would fix the wall. I couldn't find one, which made me think of all the challenges in a new light. It was time to hit the books again and make a list of the tools and materials that I would need to fix the wall.

The list was not a long one. One concern I had was the type of cement I would use to stick the rocks back together. The book said I needed some kind of mortar. I found the right stuff after I read all the cement bags at the hardware store. It was a milestone for me to find the right mortar. The next hurdle was figuring out how to mix the mortar. So, I bought a cement mixer.

When a man buys his own cement mixer, it is a big deal. I found the cheapest one I could, which meant I had to put it together. I had never put a cement mixer together before, and I did not know anyone that could help me, so I set aside a couple of hours to give the task my full attention. The instructions were in Chinese, or at least English as spoken by a Chinese person. There were not over thirty parts, and I figured it would take too long to learn Chinese, so I put the instructions back in the box and started assembling the machine.

My first attempt only took a couple of hours. The second attempt was better, it took about three and resulted in a pristine orange cement mixer. I have to say that it was one of my better assembly jobs because I used all the parts that came with the mixer and even added two of my own from my garage stash. The cement mixer worked great. I set it aside for later.

The other tools I needed were a mallet and hand chisels. The plan was to use the chisels to disassemble the wall and remove the mortar from the rocks. The mallet and chisels would get me started. I could buy the mortar when I was ready to put the wall back together.

I took photos of the wall and enlarged them. I marked each of the two hundred and seven stones in the photos with a number. I was almost ready to start disassembling the wall, when the question entered my mind of what would happen to the dirt behind the wall as I removed the stones. The wall was over three feet tall, which meant it was holding back three feet of dirt behind it. I knew it would not work to have the dirt sliding onto the sidewalk. I had talked to the city about the project to see if there was a special permit I needed. Since the plan was to not obstruct the sidewalk, other than when I was standing on the sidewalk disassembling the wall, they said I did not need a permit. I had not thought about the dirt that would bury the sidewalk as I removed the stones. The only solution I came up with was to remove the dirt from behind the wall and store it somewhere until the wall was reassembled. I put my chisels away and grabbed a shovel.

The trench turned out to be a major undertaking. Digging a thirty-foot trench, three feet deep, and twenty-four inches wide, takes a long time and results in a large pile of dirt. I did not do the math because knowing the cubic feet of dirt in the trench did nothing to make the job easier. As I dug the trench, I put the dirt in a wheelbarrow. Then I wheeled the dirt thirty yards away where I piled it out of sight under a large pine tree in the front yard. It was a clever idea because the pile of dirt was hidden from the public.

It took days to dig the trench. While digging, I was concerned that I would hit a rock that I would not be able to remove. If I did, it would indefinitely delay my wild idea until I could figure out how to remove the rock. But providence came through for me again. I only ran into one rock that weighed about one hundred pounds. After I got it dug out, it became my trophy rock. I have it prominently displayed in the backyard, a fitting reminder of the trench job. In the end, the trench turned out to be a great idea that made the job easier.

Grabbing my disassembly tools, and black magic markers, I began to remove the first rock from the wall. If there was one specific way to describe what it was like chiseling that rock out of the wall, it would be "Not Easy." I chipped around the rock for an hour or so, smacking my fingers only a couple times. I found that whatever the stuff was that was holding the wall together was strong stuff. I was finally able to get the rock freed from the wall. I was happy that the old mortar chipped off the stone easily. A check of the clock determined it took around two hours to remove one rock, and chip off the old mortar. With a magic marker I wrote the number "one" on the backside of the rock, carried the rock to the backyard where the rocks would be stored until the wall was reassembled, then I put the rock down and said, "One."

For the next few days, I continued to chisel stones from the wall. The work was hard, and it took hours to remove just three more stones. The hand chisels were not working well. While chiseling the rocks, the chisel would get snuggly stuck between the stones, requiring considerable time and muscle to remove it.

While removing stones, one of my neighbors stopped to see what I was up to. I explained how I was going to disassemble the wall and then reassemble it so that it no longer leaned. Normally, people would just nod their heads and say nothing about how crazy it was to think I could rebuild the wall like a jigsaw puzzle. Not this neighbor. He pretty much told me I was crazy. He said that there was no way to clean the mortar off the rocks; he said they would just crumble. Usually, when someone calls me crazy, I would be a little insulted. I appreciated the honesty.

Having removed the stones with my mallet and chisel, I was sure that I would not live long enough to remove all two hundred and seven stones. There had to be an easier way to do it.

A jackhammer came to mind. It seemed a jackhammer would work. I figured I could rent one, but jackhammers are pneumatic, which meant I would need to rent an air compressor too. Putting it together in my head, I knew the neighbors would not appreciate the noise I would make with the jackhammer-air compressor combo. Another problem was that I did not think it was possible to hold a jackhammer horizontally to remove the stones. Jackhammers look heavy, and when ever seeing one in use, they were always vertical.

Checking the Internet for jackhammers, I found a hammer drill. Hammer drills are electric and work like small jackhammers. The hammer drill seemed like it would be perfect for the job. It was a more expensive tool than I would normally buy, but I had to find something that would work better than the chisels. I went to the local discount tool store to see what was available.

Cheap hammer drills were selling for around three hundred dollars. The price was high for me, but in this case I did not have any choice; it was either the drill or I was left to chisel the stones out by hand. The hammer drill looked like it would work; if it did, it was worth the price.

The drill came with four types of chisels. I could not wait to try the drill. It had to work for removing the stones, or I had to go back on the hunt for another solution. I attached one of the chisels and put on my ear protection and heavy work gloves. I was happily surprised by the ease that the drill cut into the mortar between the stones. In no time at all, I removed two stones. Then the chisel broke. I was at once concerned that the drill could not manage the job. I took the chisel back to the tool store to ask the tool person if the chisel was defective or not meant for removing stones from a wall.

At the tool store, after explaining how the chisel broke and what I was using it for, the tool guy eyed me with suspicion. I thought it was a good sign. I did not want a refund, I just wanted to know if the chisel was defective or if the hammer drill could not handle the wall job.

The tool store had replacement chisels. They were expensive. I asked the tool guy if there was a warranty, and he told me that they would replace the chisel. I was thankful for the consideration, but worried that the new chisel would fail like the original one did. Back at the wall, and after several hours of chiseling stones with the new chisel, I found the chisel was just fine. The original must have been defective.

I spent the next weeks removing stones. It went much faster than doing it by hand, but it was still a time-consuming process. The hammer drill was very noisy. Not as much as a pneumatic jackhammer and compressor would have been, but it was noisy enough that I was concerned it might push one of my neighbors over the edge. I am happy to say it did not.

To add to my hammer drilling enjoyment, the temperature was around one hundred degrees the whole time. I was forced to wear my oldest cutoff shorts, an old tank top, my work boots, and a straw hat so I would not fall over from heat exhaustion. To say the least, I looked about as goofy as a circus clown. To add to my goofy look, I was covered in dust and sweat. The work was not easy, but it was good exercise. After a day working on the wall, I fully understood why those guys who run the jackhammers were in decent shape.

One issue I was concerned about was my hands. After days of working with the hammer drill, I noticed that my hands would continue to vibrate and shake after I finished. I would lie in bed at night and wonder if they would ever stop vibrating. I am happy to say that providence came through and they quit vibrating several days after I finished working on the wall.

With the way I looked, I was quite a spectacle for anyone driving by the house. The heat was so bad that I built a makeshift shelter using a tarp. It worked surprisingly good to keep the sun off me, but it also blocked any cooling breeze. I am sure people driving by thought I was a vagrant, with a hammer drill, who had set up camp on the sidewalk.

I probably should have waited for cooler weather, but I am not a waiting type of guy. I was anxious to know if I would be able to successfully complete the job.

One day, a neighbor walked across the street and asked me what I was doing. Out of breath, and very overheated, I explained that I was tearing the wall down, stone by stone, and would rebuild it so that it did not lean anymore. The only thing she could say was "Holy cow." All I could say was "Yeah, holy cow." She offered me a large fan to make the job a little more tolerable. Me, as overheated as I was, declined the offer. I am not sure why, maybe the heat had affected my judgement. But then, if my judgement was not affected, I would not have been disassembling the wall.

The best part of the story came the day I was close to removing the last stone. I noticed a fella driving by the house, obviously interested in what I was doing. I did not pay a lot of attention to him, I figured he was just someone who had never seen a vagrant with a hammer drill. Then I noticed that he parked, got out of his truck, and was walking towards me.

Being in my normal tired, hot, and dirty state, I readied myself to give another explanation. I tried to think of something to say that would make more sense than what I had been telling everyone else, but the fact was, there was no sane explanation. As the man approached, he had the look of a man with common sense. I braced myself for a judgement.

He asked me what I was doing. At that point, I had explained what I was doing to so many people, that I had my explanation memorized word for word. Looking back, I am surprised a local paper reporter did not show up to do a story about me and my project. I liked the man at once. He exuded professionalism and confidence. I explained that I was tearing the wall down because it was leaning, and that I planned to put it back together like a jigsaw puzzle. I showed him how I was numbering the stones so that I could rebuild the wall exactly as it was; only without the lean. The man looked incredulously at me, then told me he was a stonemason. I returned the incredulous look. I could not believe my ears; providence was at work yet again.

He asked me if I ever built a wall. Already suffering from wall-building -lack-of-confidence, I told him that I had not. He asked me to show him how I was planning to rebuild the wall. I showed him all the pictures of the wall that I took before starting the project, and how I had written a number on each stone so I could reassemble the wall like a puzzle. I explained, after removing and cleaning a stone, I then wrote the number that corresponded to the number on the photograph, on the back of the stone. Then I carried the stone to my backyard where I stored the stones until the time of assembly. He asked to see the stones in the backyard.

In the backyard, standing in front of two hundred stones, each with a number on it; he again looked at me incredulously again, and proclaimed that I had to be the most patient man in the world. I thought he was being kind; what he really meant was entirely another thing. I told him of my insecurity about reassembling the wall. I think it was fairly obvious, but I confessed that I did not know what I was doing. I asked him if he was interested in reassembling the wall for me. He said he would think about it and get back to me.

The next day while I was removing the last row of stones, the stonemason stopped to give me his price to rebuild the wall. After very little consideration, I told him the price was good and that I would pay him as soon as he finished rebuilding the wall.

I finished taking the wall apart and gave the stonemason the diagrams to use for reassembling the wall. Just a few days later, the stonemason and his team finished reassembling the wall to such a pristine condition that it was beyond anything I could have expected. He was truly a master stonemason.

The last part of the wall was heavy work. I had installed a water drain system behind the wall so that it would never lean again. The stonemason had partially filled the trench with rock to aid draining. I finished by adding dirt on top of the rocks and planting grass. I moved the remaining dirt to various places on the lawn and the project was finished. The wall was straight, and I would never try to straighten a wall again.

Back to the slow-dying tree. It was nice to have the tree. It provided shade and added to the ambiance of the backyard. It seemed like there were always a half dozen limbs that needed to be trimmed out each year. The branches were about eight inches in diameter and less than fifteen feet long, so other than the time it took to thread the ropes, they were easy enough to cut. It took longer to cut the Bomb Branches because I was extra careful to ensure they did not damage anything.

I cut branches off the tree for around eight years. During that time, my neighbors and friends became well acquainted with my trimming exploits. My neighbor and I talked over the fence occasionally. He is a great neighbor, and it is nice living next door to nice people like him and his wife. They could see my trimming progress from their back window, and he would occasionally comment about how a cut was going. A couple times he gave me a pat on the back for cutting an unusually difficult branch that was threatening the house or garage. They never complained about any of the wayward tennis or golf balls that fell into their yard and I tried to keep the noise to a minimum.

One day I was taking a break from cutting one of the more challenging branches. The neighbor lady was outside her house watching me. The Rope Saw was about halfway through the branch and I was sweaty, out of breath, and pretty much spent from pulling the saw for nearly an hour. Looking up at the branch, she asked me where I learned how to do that. Of course, she was referring to my Rope Saw method of cutting branches. The question struck me as very funny since I really did not think it looked like I knew what I was doing. I was so out of breath that I could barely answer, but I was able to tell her that I was learning as I went. She just said 'Oh' and then retreated back into her house.

I was glad to be providing entertainment to my neighbors. Word was also getting around to my friends about my project. They endured my stories of particularly challenging branches that I cut down. I do not think they ever really understood the gravity and danger of what I was doing, which was just fine, good friends are hard to find and if they knew the wild things I was doing they probably would have un-friended me.

One good friend, as frugal as I, mentioned that he had a particularly threatening branch between his house and the neighbor's. He was concerned that it would break off and damage either his house, the neighbor's house, or both. I told him I knew exactly what he was talking about. I could see where this was leading, so I mentioned that insurance would take care of any damage to the houses. It did not work.

He asked if I would take a look at the branch. I hinted that I did not want to lose my amateur tree trimmer status, but remembering that I had once been in the precarious position of worrying about threatening branches myself, I told him I would take a look. I admit, I was a little eager to show off my branch trimming ability. Go figure.

He was not kidding about the branch being a threatening one. It is hard to tell if a branch is in danger of breaking off or not. Most of the time a branch will break off because it cannot handle an unusually strong wind. One time a branch broke off Moby Tree during a strong storm. The branch was so large that it flattened a fifteen-foot cherry tree that it fell on. It was another display of providence because; by falling on the tree, my garage and fence were spared. The experience made me suspicious of branches. I knew they could turn on you at any time.

The branch was within ten feet of the neighbor's house and ten feet of my friend's house. It was a good-sized branch, and it was a Bomb Branch. We stood in his yard looking up at the branch while I thought of ways to avoid committing to cutting the branch down. Since it was a bomb branch, I would have to tie the branch to a Security Branch so that the Target Branch could be guided safely to the ground. Out of the kindness of my heart, and an ego as big as the tree in my backyard, I retrieved my Rope Saw paraphernalia out of the pickup and set up to start lobbing golf balls.

To make a long story short, I was able to route all the lines quickly because the branches were pretty much clear of obstructions. The branch was about forty feet up in the tree, so it was not a small feat. The cut went perfectly, and my friend was amazed as I lowered the limb safely to the ground using the Security Line. I cut the branch up into manageable chunks and the job was done. Of course, there was no way I would charge my friend anything for the work, thereby saving my amateur tree trimmer status. After praising my stellar performance, my friend thanked me and asked me if I was interested in trimming the rest of the trees in his yard. I graciously declined the offer.

It was nice being able to help someone with what I had learned. All the details of my Rope Saw method were working, except for the golf ball throwing. It was a bad link in an almost perfect method. I had to find a better way.

8
The Release

Throwing the golf ball was working, but not good enough. It always took many throws to route a line over a branch. The weight of the golf ball was perfect. The weight made the ball fall to the ground almost every time I threw it into the tree. The tennis ball just did not have enough weight, which caused it to hang up more often. The tennis ball would also bounce around when it hit the branches and that would cause me to miss the mark or would cause the line to become tangled among the branches. When the line got tangled, it took a lot of time to get the ball back to the ground for another throw. The golf ball reduced the time needed to thread a line because it often just fell through the branches back to the ground. I could cut the line from it and easily pull the line back to the ground.

I could not stop thinking that there had to be a way to accurately throw the golf ball. I could not get the archery idea out of my head. Maybe it was because most of my archery shooting was target shooting.

I was not an outstanding target shooter, but I was able to put arrows into respectable groups. Knowing that accuracy was possible with a bow and arrow kept me thinking that there had to be a better way to shoot a golf ball accurately.

My best ideas come to me during stretches of insomnia while laying in bed holding my eyes shut. I have often thought I should turn in the time for pay, since I have solved some of the biggest problems at work during those times. At least the boss could allow some nap time during my shift so I could recoup a little desperately needed rest. I did mention it once. Bosses never see things my way.

There is a good chance I was standing in the backyard looking up at the tree when I finally figured it out. The idea was so obvious once I thought of it, that I was a little embarrassed that I had spent so much time trying to shoot the golf ball by holding it with my fingers.

The idea was simple. I would cut a small slit in the leather (see Figure 130a) on my slingshot (see Figure 130b), into which I could insert the eyehook (see Figure 131a). I could then grasp the eyehook with my mechanical archery release (see Figure 131b and 132a).

The slingshot could be drawn back like a bow, aimed, and the golf ball released by squeezing the mechanical archery release trigger (see Figure 132b). It is unusual for me, but my first inclination was that there was no way it would work. I thought the eyehook would not pass smoothly through the slit in the leather of the slingshot, which would cause the shot to do something completely unexpected; maybe even cause an injury. With apprehension I prepared to test the idea.

Cutting the slit in the slingshot leather was a little touchy. I didn't want to make the cut too large in case it wrecked the leather, neither could it be too small so that the eyehook fit into it too snuggly. If the eyehook fit too tightly, it would not be freely released from the leather and would result in knocking one of my eyes out, so I cut the slit with that in mind.

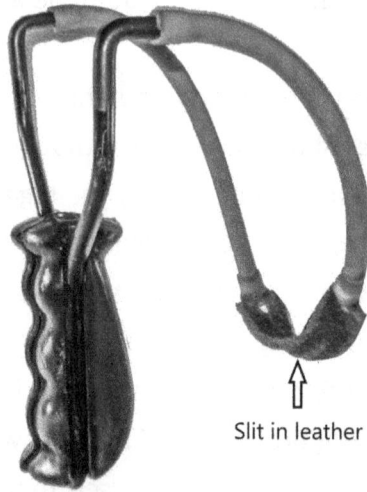

Slit in leather

Figure 130a

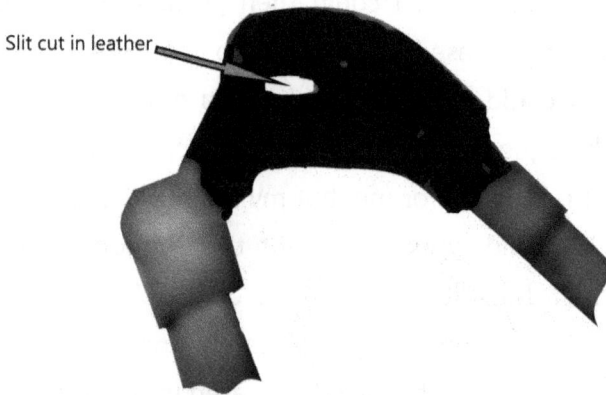

Slit cut in leather

Figure 130b

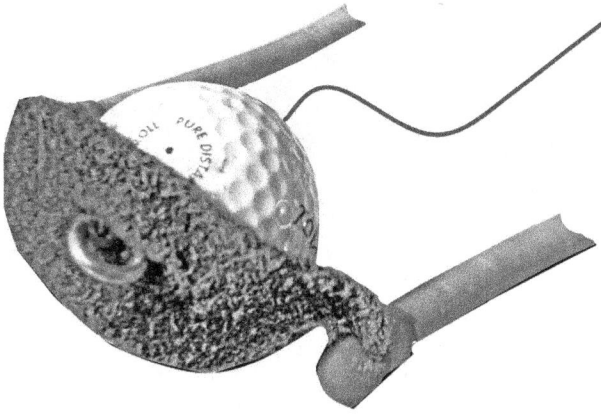

Figure 131a

Figure 131b

Figure 132a

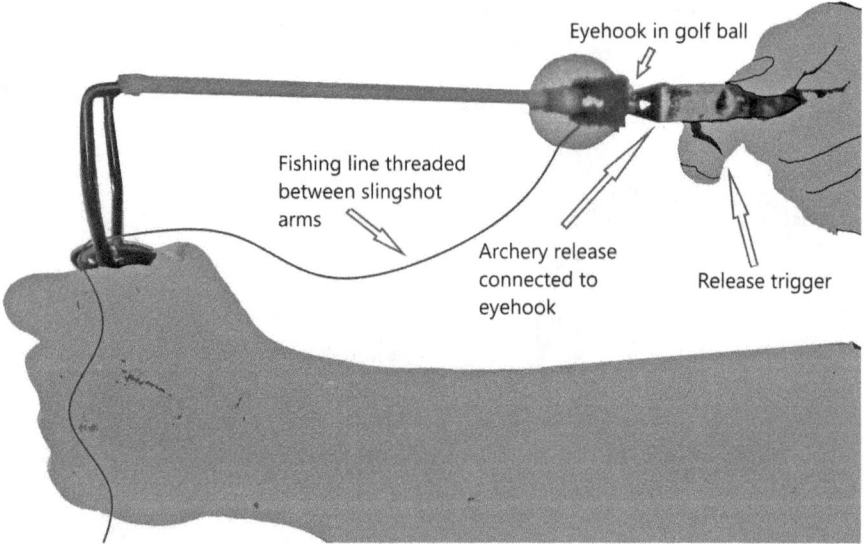

Eyehook in golf ball

Fishing line threaded
between slingshot
arms

Archery release
connected to
eyehook

Release trigger

Figure 132b

The next issue was to ensure the string did not get tangled in the slingshot when the ball was shot. The only difference from the non-archery release method, was that the string might be affected because it was pushed through the slit in the leather with the eyehook. Another concern was what the string did when pulling the slingshot back; would It create a little slack that could become a snag danger. If the string hanging between the slingshot arms and the golf ball became tangled, it could have resulted in an injury as well. I always disliked testing dangerous stuff, but there are ways to avoid danger.

For the test, I first made a hip shot. I did not aim. I just wanted to see if the slingshot would shoot the ball smoothly. I knew how far to pull the slingshot back so that the ball did not fly too far.

I drew the sling shot back, pointing it so it would not damage anything, and let the ball fly. It worked; smoothly. I tried it a half-dozen more times and the ball always freely released from the slingshot and went freely through the air. It looked like the idea was going to work.

Next, I tested the sling shot by holding it normally and aiming between the slingshot arms at the target. I was careful to ensure the eyehook was positioned correctly in the leather and that the fishing line lay freely between the slingshot arms.   The first shot I took was an easy shot. The shot worked perfectly and traveled a good distance. Next, I aimed at the branch I wanted to cut next. The branch was about forty feet up and did not have any branches that would interfere with the shot. I let the golf ball fly and hit the target on the first shot. I was delighted. After two years of burning time flinging tennis balls and golf balls into the tree, I had a precise way to shoot a line over a branch. The time savings would be significant, my Rope Saw method was perfected. Now I know what Einstein felt like when he figured out that mass speed of light thing.

There was one added concern with the slingshot. The slingshot instructions said the rubbers on the slingshot needed to be checked occasionally to ensure they were not in danger of breaking; causing injury to the user.

9
Easy Street

I named this chapter Easy Street; compared with the initial Rope Saw Archery Method, this new Archery Method was like living on easy street. Through the experience of using the Rope Saw, there were a multitude of challenges I was able to find workable solutions to. The greatest challenge was the time it took to get the ropes routed. The Archery Method resolved that issue completely. I found using the Rope Saw was anything but a simple matter. Cutting branches with a Rope Saw requires diligence and the use of extreme caution to avoid physical harm and damage to structures. I was Blessed that I was able to learn how to use the Rope Saw without injuring myself or anything else.

I continued to trim the tree as the branches died. Each year there were at least five new branches to remove. Using the Archery Method I was able to quickly route lines and get things set up to cut a branch. One issue that I was not able to overcome consistently was how to extract the Rope Saw when it became stuck in a cut. What worked best;

was to avoid getting the saw stuck in the first place. To avoid getting the saw stuck, I did not pull too hard on the Rope Saw as it cut. It was always a temptation to pull the saw hard so that it would bite into the wood better and cut faster, but that was a mistake. It took longer to cut, but it was better to just let the weight of the saw make the cut. If I could see sawdust falling from the cut, I knew it was cutting.

What happened is that, when the saw was not pulled too hard, the cut was wider because the saw was able to jump around in the cut, making it wider. Because the cut was wider, the saw was less likely to stick. When pulling hard, the cut was only as wide as the saw. Just like sawing a branch with a tree saw, if the sawing is too fast the saw starts to stick. It took me longer to make a cut, but because I was not pulling so hard, it was not any more strenuous than quickly cutting the branch by hard-pulling.

I found too, that the branch I was cutting made a significant difference. The Archery Method allowed me to trim branches much faster, which gave me more time to remove branches that were dead, but low priorities because they were not threatening the house or garage.

One branch was about eight feet long and a foot thick with no secondary branches on it. Because the branch did not have any secondary branches on it, it was easy to shoot both the Security Line and the Rope Saw Lines over it. I used a Security Line because I thought it would be too heavy to just let it drop to the ground. After two shots with the slingshot everything was set up for the cut. It was all straightforward and worked perfectly. Unfortunately, it turned into one of the hardest cuts of all my Rope Saw experiences. I refer to the branch as "The Mule".

One of the most crucial details of using the Rope Saw was that the Rope Saw Line's connection point to the Rope Saw had to be checked each time I used the Rope Saw. The Rope Saw Line connections could not appear frayed or worn (see Figure 138a).

After using the Rope Saw for awhile the Rope Saw Lines became worn and frayed (see Figure 138b and 138c). If the Rope Saw Lines became worn and frayed, they could break from the Rope Saw while I was making a cut. If a line broke while making a cut, it was difficult to retrieve the Rope Saw. It was always best to retie the Rope Saw Line when it became frayed or worn to the point of breakage. Whenever I was in doubt, I retied the lines.

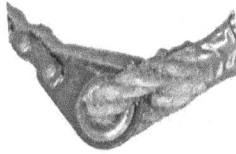

Figure 138a

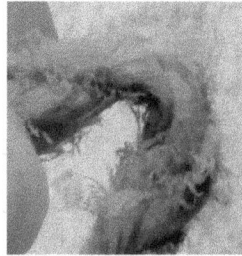

Figure 138b   Figure 138c

10
The Mule

The first issue I ran into with the Mule was that the saw stuck. I was careful not to pull the saw too hard while cutting, but it did not make any difference. I think the reason was because the branch, which was only about eight feet long, was originally much longer. I had cut off the end as one of the first test cuts, so the heavy end of the branch was missing. There was no down force at the end of the branch to help pull the cut open as I cut, and so the cut snugged around the Rope Saw and it became stuck. Really stuck.

When the Rope Saw became stuck, I was careful not to force it into the cut further by pulling hard on the lines to free it. I would lightly snap the Rope Saw alternately on each side to try to loosen it. If I was able to loosen it, I could begin pulling it lightly again to continue cutting. These steps did not work with the Mule, so I set up to use the Saver Method outlined, beginning on page 90, to extract the saw from the cut.

For the Mule, it was difficult to set up the Saver Method because the only Utility Branches that could be used were not directly over the Mule. To be most effective, the Utility Branch for the Saver Method needs to be as directly over the stuck Rope Saw as possible. Because the Utility Branch was not directly above the cut, the carabiner could not pull the Rope Saw straight up and out of the cut. Instead, it ineffectively pulled the Rope Saw to the side. I tried running the carabiner up the other Rope Saw Line with the same outcome. This saw was really stuck. I already had a rusty old Rope Saw stuck in the tree. I was not happy about having two. At that point I began a frustrating journey to try to retrieve the newly stuck Rope Saw.

The first thing I did was violate my own rule. I tried as hard as possible to pull the Rope Saw so that it would free up and begin cutting. It was really stuck before, but now even more stuck. I was quite sure it was stuck beyond unsticking. But I am not one to give up.

I am not sure how long I worked trying to free the saw. I snapped it, pulled it, and tried the Saver Method again. I even considered putting my twenty-foot ladder on top of the garage and extending it up to the tree where the saw was at. It would have put me almost thirty feet in the air with nothing to keep the ladder steady. Fortunately, I kept my wits about me and trashed the idea.

The next thing I did, confirms that I do not follow my own advice. I tried to pull the saw strongly to free it and start it cutting again. Pulling as hard as I could, I got the saw to move about half an inch. After what I had been through, this was clearly progress. I was overjoyed, which proves it does not take much to make me happy.

I started pulling the Rope Saw, alternately right to left. I was moving the Rope Saw a small distance each way. I knew if I could keep doing it, the distance would eventually increase, and the Rope Saw would be back to cutting the branch normally.

Pulling the Rope Saw one half inch was not easy. It was much easier if the saw moved smoothly and at a normal distance. When the distance was so short, there was a tendency to pull too hard, and that is what I did. Then the grand nightmare of Rope Saw users happened; one of the Rope Saw Lines broke.

Before I started the cut, I checked the Rope Saw Lines for wear and fraying. But, because the line broke it was clear that it must have been too worn, or maybe I just pulled too hard. In any case, the Rope Saw was stuck and now had only one rope connected to it. There was no way to alternately pull the Rope Saw anymore. The Rope Saw hung ominously in the tree, and it looked like it would be there for awhile.

I retried the Saver Method. I thought the Rope Saw would be easier to remove now because it had only one rope connected to it. I am not sure what is logical about that, it is probably the same logic a deer uses when he sees headlights and decides to just stop to see what happens. The saw, of course, did not budge. I needed a whole new idea. Which turned out to be a bad one.

This was about my eighth year using the Rope Saw. Everyone reaches a point where they give up. I was not there yet. I looked up at the branch with the saw hanging there with only one line attached. I admit, it looked as hopeless as any challenge I had seen with the saw so far. I had no idea what I would do at this point. So I settled on trying to figure out how to disconnect the other rope from the saw. Although I had not made the decision yet, I was leaning toward abandoning the second Rope Saw in the tree.

Getting the other Rope Saw Line off the Rope Saw would not be an easy task. I had a couple of ideas; one was to somehow get my propane torch up to the line to burn it off. The ropes are very tough and not easy to cut. Even though the one Rope Saw Line broke, I knew I would not be able to break off the other line by pulling it. I quickly trashed the propane torch idea. I had visions of starting the tree on fire, which, although it would be nice to be rid of the tree, would likely open a whole new list of problems.

My next idea was to run a small saw up on a utility line using another utility line, but there was no way to manipulate the saw once it reached the connection. The Rope Saw was about thirty feet from the ground. My third and last idea was to cut the branch closer to the tree with a new Rope Saw. If I could do that, the stuck Rope Saw would fall to the ground with the branch. I ordered another Rope Saw; it was the third Rope Saw I bought.

It would take about a week for my new Rope Saw to arrive. I knew that even with the new Rope Saw, it would be tricky to cut the branch down because the stuck Rope Saw was too close to where the branch joined the tree. I would have to place the new Rope Saw somewhere between the stuck Rope Saw and where the branch joined the tree. It did not give me much of a target. Even if I was able to place the saw correctly, with all the conditions the same as when the first Rope Saw stuck, it was likely the new Rope Saw would become stuck as well. With that in mind, I came up with yet, another idea; which was one of my worst ideas of all time.

The cut in the branch was a little over halfway through the branch. I thought, if there was a way that I could pull hard enough on the branch to break it off at the cut, then the branch would be out of the tree and the Rope Saw would fall to the ground. If the Rope Saw did not fall to the ground, it would likely be easier to retrieve with the cut being broken open. The challenge was how to pull on the branch hard enough to make it break.

The first thing I did was shoot a rope over the end of the branch. The slingshot worked so well that it took only one shot. I attached a carabiner to the rope to make a hangman's knot and attached a safety line to the carabiner in case I needed to back out of the procedure. I pulled the hangman's knot tight around the branch and physically tried to pull and break the branch by pulling on the utility line, but even after using my full weight, the branch would not break (see Figure 144).

Attempting to
break branch to
free Rope Saw

Stuck Rope Saw

Carabiner
Safety Line

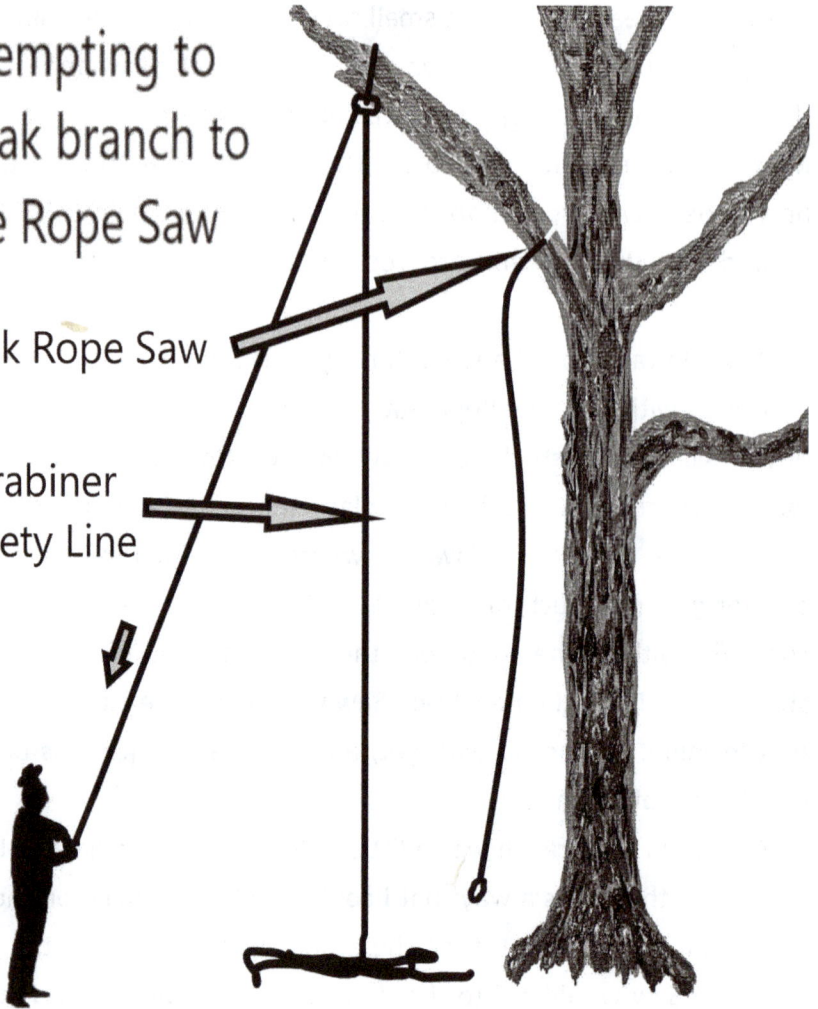

Figure 144

Putting my full weight on the branch was a ridiculously wild thing to do. If the branch had broken, I would never have had enough time to bolt from under it before it injured me. This was one of the most dangerous things I ever did while cutting branches. I believe it illustrates how desperation can drive us to take dangerous chances.

Realizing the branch was not going to come down easily, it was time for another idea. I was hoping it would not be as wild as the last. Unfortunately, it was worse.

Years previously, I had an idea that proved to be undoable. However, I did not realize it until after I tried it. I thought the idea would work, and it did not seem to be at all dangerous.

It all started early one morning while I was eating breakfast. As I was enjoying my daily bowl of oatmeal, I glanced out at the privacy fence in the backyard. To my horror it was flopping side to side in the wind. The posts were not broken off, they were just loosened by the wind so the fence would lean back and forth as the wind blew.

After breakfast I hurried out to see what my next challenge was going to be. It did not look good. Three fence posts had been worked loose by the strong wind. The "not good" part was that the posts were set in concrete. I had absolutely no experience with fences and particularly no experience working with five-by-five wooden fence posts that were set in concrete.

The wooden posts would need to be replaced, so I formulated a plan. I would replace each post, one at a time. I would remove the old one, then replace it with a new one and secure it to the fence. After all the wooden posts were replaced, the fence would be firm and able to withstand any high winds. The plan would take days, and although I was not aware of it at the time, would not go smoothly.

I disconnected the posts from the fence. Cutting the multiple nails that attached the posts to the fence was a challenge. The prior owner of my house owned a hardware store, which explained why they were able to use so many nails. I knew that pounding nails in is always easier than pulling them out, and disconnecting the posts from the fence proved that I was right.

Once I had the first post detached from the fence, I thought it would be a simple matter to slide the post out of the concrete that was anchoring it in the ground. It made sense because the fence was wobbling back and forth. It did not occur to me that the concrete was loosened or maybe the fence post was cracked. To this day I am not sure what was allowing the fence to wobble. It did not matter, there was no way I could pull the post out of the concrete. I tried to do it by hand and that did not work. Then I tried nailing a good-sized board to the side of the post so I could put a car jack under the board and jack the post out. That did not work either, but it confirmed that the post was in the concrete tight and that I was not going to pull it out.

The next thing I did was get out my trusty hammer drill. The drill had meritoriously helped me dismantle the wall; I figured I could now use it to remove the concrete from the post. I dug deep into the ground to reveal the concrete that was holding the post in the ground. I could not get down too far, but I could see the top of the concrete, so I started hammer drilling the concrete to break the post free. With significant effort, I was able to break small chunks off the concrete. Progress was slow, minimal, and I did not really care because it was easier than digging.

After a couple of hours of making almost no progress, my hands were beginning to tingle again from using the hammer drill. It became clear to me that the hammer drill was not going to do the job. Dynamite came to mind, but I was sure I did not have any in the garage, which was a good thing.

I did have a crowbar, which I used to attempt to move and loosen the concrete around the post. The concrete was not moving even the tiniest bit. I was completely mystified as to how the post could wobble and yet be solidly embedded in the concrete. No matter, I had to come up with something. The fence had to be fixed.

As unlikely as it sounds, I thought there might be a way that I could lift the concrete out of the hole. Obviously, I was not strong enough to do it by hand. I would need something with more strength. Buying a backhoe crossed my mind, but I had nowhere to store it. If I did, it is where I would have parked my boat instead of taking it to the dealers to be sold on consignment.

I have a long history of getting stuck with my vehicles. Where I live, the snow gets deep in the winter and the mud gets deep in the Spring. I have experienced being stuck in both. The one essential tool, for someone who gets stuck often, is a come along tool. To use a come along tool when you get stuck, you connect a chain or tow rope to your vehicle, then you connect the chain or tow rope to the come along tool which is connected by a chain or tow rope to some stationary object. Then you crank the come along tool to winch the vehicle free from being stuck. The only thing that can foil a come along tool is if you are too far away from any stationary object. I have been. Once a tow truck had to hook two one-hundred-foot cables together to pull me out of a swamp.

I had a come along tool in my garage. All I needed now was something to hook it to so the concrete could be lifted out of the hole. That was a problem. There was nothing to hook it to. What I ended up doing was reattaching the post to the fence, and then near each loose post I set another post as close as I could to it. The project took days, was not as bad as the wall project, but was every bit as hard. The whole point of the story is the come along tool was still in my garage. Using it, I would be able to apply much more force to the branch.

Looking back through the years, using the come along tool to try breaking the branch from the tree was one of the most dangerous things I have done. It makes me shiver a little just thinking about it.

I had a Rope Saw stuck in the tree with one of the lines broken from it. I could not think of a way to free the Rope Saw. I also knew it was not safe for me to continue thinking up innovative ideas, because they were getting increasingly wilder. What I was about to do was absolutely an act of final desperation.

I thought the rope that I attached to the end of the Target Branch

147

was strong enough to break the branch. The plan was to connect the come along tool to the rope and then wrap another rope around the trunk of the tree and connect it to the come along tool (see Figure 148). I would then tighten the come along tool to apply energy to the end of the branch and break it off. The come along tool could pull a four-thousand-pound stuck vehicle out of snowbanks and bogs. It should be able to break the branch.

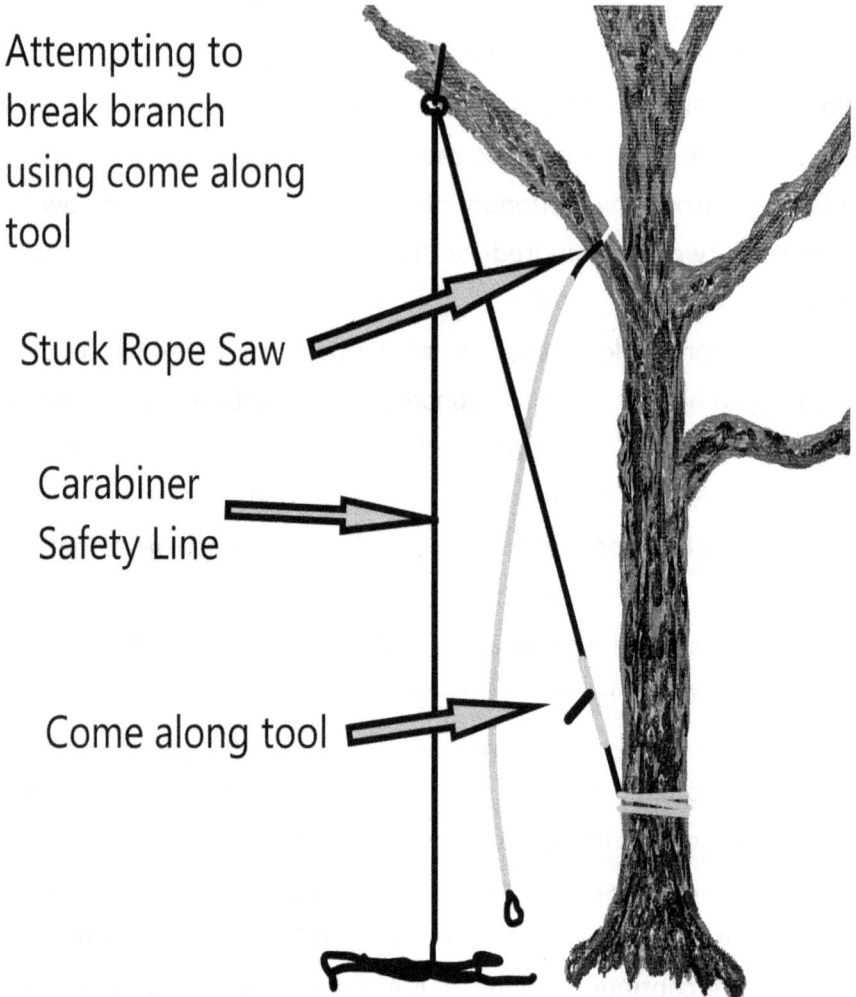

Attempting to break branch using come along tool

Stuck Rope Saw

Carabiner Safety Line

Come along tool

Figure 148

I positioned the come along tool so that I would have minimal exposure should the rope break and snap back at me. This idea was one of my riskiest, and I needed to be as careful as possible. I thought the rope I was using was strong enough to withstand the tension of the come along tool and the force needed to break the branch, but I knew how dense and tough the branches were and I knew the tension needed to break the branch would be extreme.

I connected the come along tool to the rope attached to the end of the branch, and then connected it to the rope I had wound around the tree. The angle that the come along tool would pull the branch was not the best, but it looked good enough to break the branch. I began tightening the come along tool. The rope tightened up quickly and, as it did, ratchetting the come along tool got harder to do. I continued tightening it by reaching around the tree and pulling on the come along tool handle. The tension on the rope was increasing rapidly. I stopped to recheck everything to make sure nothing could go wrong.

Tightening the come along tool was stressful. The tension of the rope was concerning. I was not sure if the rope would break and snap back at me. If the rope held, and the branch broke, I was concerned what would happen when it did. There was nothing the branch would hit and damage, but the force was so great on the rope that I was not sure what would happen.

I continued tightening the tool. The rope was becoming super taught to a point that I feared the rope would break. Yet the branch made no noise or gave any sign that it was going to break off. I stopped again to consider what would happen if the branch broke and what exactly I could expect from the very heavy projectile racing toward the ground near where I was standing. I continued to tighten the come along tool.

There is a point in any action, when we know, something is about to happen. In the case of this procedure with the come along tool, I was fast approaching that point. I felt the come along tool was nearing its maximum tightness point. Standing beneath the limb while tightening the come along tool, was a stressful time. I had to decide whether I should continue tightening it to the point where something happened, or if I should stop. I ducked behind the tree trunk again and grasped the come along tool. Pulling the come along tool was difficult. I pulled the lever until I could hear the slow clicking of the cogs as they locked the rope into an even tighter state. I stopped, waited, then pulled the lever again until I heard three more clicks. Then I stopped.

I had enough. For over eight years I had battled the tree limbs. I risked my safety and worked until I could almost work no more. All the branches I needed to remove had been removed, except for the Mule. For years, the one rusted Rope Saw hung in the tree. It was still there. Now it was joined by another Rope Saw, one that had one line still connected to it. A new Rope Saw was on its way from the seller, but I did not have any more desire to continue cutting branches.

Unlike Captain Ahab, I would not continue to tighten the come along tool to the point that I went down with Moby Tree as Captain Ahab went down with Moby Dick. I felt an uneasy foreboding while I was giving the come along tool the last few pulls. For one of the first times in my life, I would heed the warning. I declared that trimming the tree was complete. There was only one thing left to do. I carefully loosened the come along tool, removed the ropes from the branch, tied the lone Rope Saw Line as out of sight as possible around the tree, went into the house, and called a tree service to ask them for a cost estimate to cut the tree down.

11
The Rubicon

Julius Caesar decided to cross the Rubicon River in 49 BC. The Rubicon was a restricted boundary, and Caesar knew that once crossed, there was no turning back. Similarly, I realized that calling the tree service was my Rubicon; there would be no turning back.

I must admit, I felt relief when I made the decision. Trimming the tree through the years was perhaps the hardest work I have done in my life. The dying branches were a constant cloud hanging over me for eight years. The tree had pushed me to my limit, the final straw was the Mule, a stuck saw, and a come along tool stressed to its limit.

The owner of the tree service said he would stop by the next day for a look. For just a moment, I thought I should at least disconnect the one Rope Saw Line from the stuck Rope Saw. I thought it would be a little less embarrassing. I began to formulate exactly how I was going to explain the two Rope Saws that were stuck in the tree. For a moment I thought maybe he wouldn't notice them, even though one still had the yellow rope connected. It would be better if I could get the Rope Saw Line disconnected from the Rope Saw, but I had crossed the Rubicon. Embarrassed or not, I would not touch the tree again.

The next day the tree guy showed up right on time. Let's say his name is Rex. That is not his real name, I just do not want to start anything between him and the first tree service guy. I did not call the first tree service guy because it would be too much crow to eat.

It crossed my mind that because I had removed so many of the branches from the tree, the price to take the tree down would be less. But, even if the price was less, the first tree guy said I would have to take down the fence and the awning in order for him to cut the tree down. I was sure he would still require me to do that, and after my experience fixing the wind-loosened-fence, there was no way I would consider taking the fence down. Taking the awning down would have been a whole new adventure, and I was not looking for any new adventures; in fact, I was looking forward to no adventures.

Rex was the real meat and potatoes tree trimming type. I could tell right away that he had experience trimming trees. Jed was more the business type who did not actually trim the trees, but he had a great crew who did. Rex was a real leader; he led his crew into battle and did the major cutting himself. He was like Custer, only he trimmed trees. I liked him the first time I met him.

The time leading up to a bid is always tense for me. I was hoping for a good bid; better than the last one, and Rex's attitude was positive. He spoke directly and openly. His first comment was "Man, that's a big tree", which is exactly what Jed had said. It kind of amazed me because, if it was not a big tree, I would have been able to hack it down myself. In any case, it did not bother me because I knew it was a big tree.

I wanted to get the embarrassing part out of the way as soon as I could. So, I explained how I had been trimming branches with a Rope Saw for the last eight years. Rex did not seem surprised at all, which confirmed that his level of tree trimming experience was vast. I showed him where the rusty Rope Saw was stuck, and unnecessarily pointed out the recently stuck Rope Saw with the yellow rope attached. As Rex looked up at the stuck saws, I could tell he wanted to say something, but he held back because he was dealing with a paying customer.

Rex scanned the backyard looking at the fence, the garage, and the awning. Then he walked around the tree a couple times. Then what he said was music to my ears. He said, because of the fence, he would need to use a crane to remove the tree. I thought, if I had a crane, there would not be any wild idea too big for me. This Rex guy was sharp! Of course, I asked him if he had a crane. He did not. But he said he could hire one, and that they cost about two hundred and fifty dollars an hour. I quickly compared the rate with what I was making at my job and concluded those crane guys do good.

I hesitated, but just to make sure, I asked about any need to remove the fence or awning. He said that there was not any need to mess with them. I liked that. Rex told me he would get the bid to me as soon as he could.

The next day Rex stopped by, which was a good sign. It seemed he would have called if the bid was high. Rex and I hung around the tree some more. Rex gave the tree a couple more professional tree service glances, then he gave me the bid. He said it would come to around five thousand dollars; depending on how long he had to rent the crane. I told him I would pay him when he finished the job.

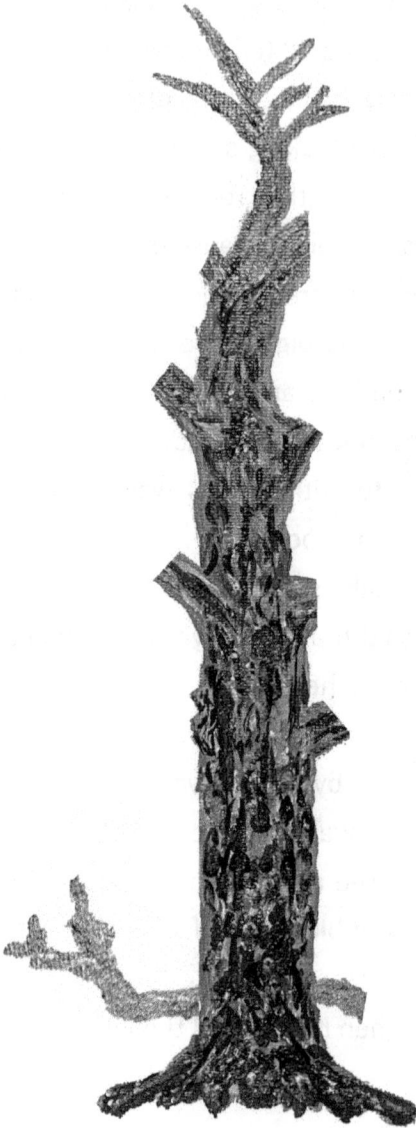

12
Goodbye Moby

The day was pleasantly warm with a light breeze. Shortly after sunrise the crane pulled up and began to unload. At about the same time Rex and his crew showed up. The crane operator began to set up in the alley, putting down the crane's long anchor arms to keep it from tipping over. Rex's vehicles lined up along the street in front of the house with others parked in the alley near the crane.

Rex was in a good mood. It was easy to tell he liked his job and was looking forward to the challenge ahead. I greeted Rex and let him know that I would be grilling hamburgers with the works for the crew's noon lunch.

In no time at all, one of Rex's men began scaling the tree, started tying off branches, and had begun cutting them off. It was a thing of beauty to see professionals who knew what they were doing. I kept my distance lest someone ask me about one of the stuck Rope Saws.

As I watched the crane hoist the branches over the garage, I cannot say I was sorry to see the tree going. I had really had enough.

There was still much of the tree to cut at lunch time. I grilled up two dozen hamburgers with buns, served up potato salad, chips, and ice-cold water and sodas. Everyone was in good spirits. They were men who enjoyed working hard and the size of the tree made it a special challenge.

It was near four in the afternoon when they cut off the last two large branches from the tree. The trucks in the alley and in front of the house were loaded with wood from the tree. I walked to the front of the house and found the branches with the Rope Saws stuck in them. The thought crossed my mind to try to retrieve them, but then, I decided to let them go with the tree. I had a new saw on the way and had no use for either of the two stuck saws. I was thinking Rex would retrieve them and incorporate them into his business. I imagined seeing one of his trucks pull up in front of a house and the tree guy getting out with one of the Rope Saws.

I returned to the backyard where I found Rex making the final cut of the trunk. The only remaining part of the tree was the trunk and two of the main branches reaching into the air. As the crane lifted the heart of the tree away, it looked to me like the tree was beckoning providence for mercy, and yet was thankful for all the time it had stood majestically in the backyard.

When we return from an adventure, we often reflect on the experiences we had during the adventure. My Rope Saw adventure lasted longer than I could have imagined. It was challenging, dangerous, and difficult work from the start.

It started because I wanted to save money, yet after all the work, the cost remained exactly the same as before I started. It was not a wasted adventure. I learned how to use a Rope Saw, and I learned a valuable lesson that I will never forget; Dad was right.

The End

Glossary

Archery Method: The method using a mechanical archery release to shoot a golf ball with a slingshot.

Bomb Branch: A branch that will damage a structure if it is allowed to free fall from a tree.

Carabiner Safety Line: A line attached to a carabiner that is used to pull the carabiner back to the ground.

Crawl Walk Run Method: The method of moving slowly while a new project is learned.

David's Slingshot Method: Throwing a tennis ball by twirling the line attached to it and releasing it at the precise time so that the tennis ball hits the intended target.

Flip Tab: A flat metal tab on the Rope Saw Line that flips the teeth of the Rope Saw down, facing the branch, when it strikes the branch as it is being pulled over it.

Free Fall Branch: A branch that will not damage any structures if it is allowed to fall from the tree.

Moby Tree: The name given to the subject tree of this book.

Offset Security Branch: A branch that is not directly above a Target Branch that is used to suspend the Target Branch while moving it away from any structures after it is cut from the tree.

Rope Saw Line: One of two ropes attached to the Rope Saw.

Saver Method: Method used to lift a Rope Saw out of the cut it is making.

Security Branch: A branch a Security Line is routed over.

Security Line: A line routed over a Security Branch that is connected to a

Target Branch so that the Target Branch remains suspended after it is cut from the tree.

Spiral Cut: A cut that is being made at different angles on each side of a branch.

Stepladder Rake Maneuver: The method of retrieving a tennis or golf ball that is hanging out of reach.

Target Offset Method: The highest inset spliced, can, on placement yellow rope, indicate general high targets below each length. On nearest good side, tie on fixed lengths on your drop pieces, and retie sturdy knot.

Target Branch: the branch that is currently selected to be cut from a tree.

Tennis Ball Method: Using a tennis ball to throw a line over a branch.

Mule: A branch that is impossible to cut free from a tree.

Utility Branch: A branch used to support a Utility Line.

Utility Line: A rope used as part of the Save Method to lift a rope saw from a cut, or ropes whose use is not specifically defined.

ABOUT THE AUTHOR

Floyd Roland Park retired from the South Dakota Highway Patrol before earning a Computer Science degree from the South Dakota School of Mines and Technology. Passionate about software development since 1985, Floyd has been a professional software engineer since 2008. His diverse career includes roles as a systems and network administrator and software developer for the United States Air Force, a technical writer for a contracting company, and a software developer for a school district. Now retired, Floyd enjoys writing for fun, sharing stories and experiences drawn from a life rich in diverse pursuits and professional expertise.

Credits

Rights to use the tree image found on the title page, dedication page, and pages 1, 11, 25, 44, 63, 96, 111, 128, 136, 140, 152, and 157 purchased from Shutterstock, Inc. Empire State Building 350 Fifth Avenue, 21st Floor, New York, NY 10118

Rights to use the whale image found on page 158 purchased from Shutterstock, Inc. Empire State Building 350 Fifth Avenue, 21st Floor, New York, NY 10118

Photographs found on pages 32, 33, 35, 51, 52, 53, 54, 55, 56, 57, 58, 59, 60, 61, 62, 67, 76, 101, 113, 122, 130, 131, 132, and 138 are from the author's personal collection.

www.ingramcontent.com/pod-product-compliance
Lightning Source LLC
Chambersburg PA
CBHW070205060426
42445CB00033B/1540